iBT b TOEFL LISTENING
NEW EDITION

LinguaForum

기획	링구아포럼 기획편집팀
지은이	링구아포럼 리서치센터 연구팀
디자인	링구아포럼 디자인팀
편집인	최인호
발행인	이길호
발행처	링구아포럼
1판4쇄	2014. 12. 26
교재문의	02) 3480-6613　　대표전화 02) 590-6900
등록번호	제2000-000335호　　등록일자 2000. 5. 17　　ISBN 978-89-5563-628-4 (14740)　　가격 19,000원

Copyright © 2010-2011 by LinguaForum

No unauthorized photocopying.

All rights reserved. No part of this book may be reproduced or transmitted in any form or by any means, electronic or mechanical, including photocopying, recording, or any other information storage and retrieval system without the written permission of the publisher.
이 책은 링구아포럼이 독창적으로 개발하였습니다. 이 책의 내용, 사진 등 일부 혹은 전체 내용을 어떠한 방법으로도 무단 복사, 복제, 전재하는 것은 저작권법에 의해 금지되어 있습니다.

Printed in the Republic of Korea *ss1605*

R/N(CRbTFLneG): 09301030KB / 12071030KB / 03301130KB

머리말

1990년대 이후부터 우리나라 영어교육에서 청취력에 관한 관심이 학교의 현장 교육, 교재 개발 및 평가 반영 등의 분야에서 높게 나타나고 있음에도 불구하고 청취에 관련된 기본 지침서나 교재 등이 부족했던 것이 현실이다. 더욱이 TOEFL과 관련된 초·중급 수준 교재의 빈약함에 대한 학습자들의 고충을 덜어보려는 노력으로 LinguaForum Research Center에서는 초·중급용 청취 교재를 개발하게 되었다.

청취는 짧은 시간 내에 일정한 실력을 쌓기가 쉽지 않은 일이긴 하지만, 훌륭한 방법론을 제시한 좋은 교재로 학습해 나간다면 못할 일도 아니다. 청취는 영어의 다른 분야와 마찬가지로 매일 학습하는 것이 필요하며, 가능하다면 청취에 항상 개방된 자세와 환경의 유지가 무엇보다도 필요하다.

이번에 새로운 디자인과 구성으로 개정한 링구아포럼 iBT b TOEFL Listening은 중급 수준에 최적화된 교재로서 TOEFL 청취 전반을 학습할 수 있도록 구성하였다. 특히 iBT TOEFL 문제 유형의 개념 정리부터 실전용 Test에 이르기까지 흐름을 알기 쉽게 정리해 놓았다.

아무쪼록 링구아포럼에서 만든 본 교재가 학습자들의 기본적인 영어 이해 능력과 의사소통 능력 신장에 도움을 주고 독자들이 소기의 목적을 이룰 수 있다면, 저희는 더할 나위 없는 보람으로 여기며 보다 나은 책을 만들어 내는데 정진 할 것을 약속한다.

LinguaForum Research Center
청취 연구팀

Structure

각 장의 구성

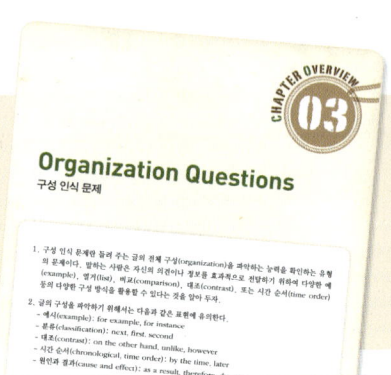

Overview

*i*BT TOEFL의 각 문제 유형에 대한 중요 사항을 설명하며 문제 풀이에 필요한 정보를 제공한다.

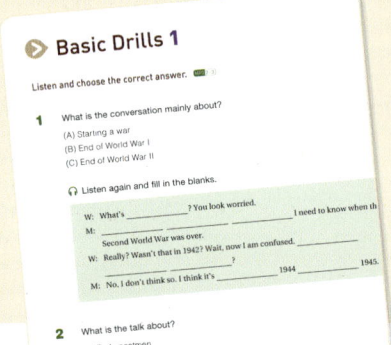

Basic Drills

본격적인 청취 연습에 앞서 각 장에서 소개한 토플 문제 유형에 대한 기본 개념을 짧은 청취 지문을 통해 연습한다. 뿐만 아니라 토플 청취 영역에서 중요한 노트테이킹을 연습함으로써 실전에 활용할 수 있도록 한다.

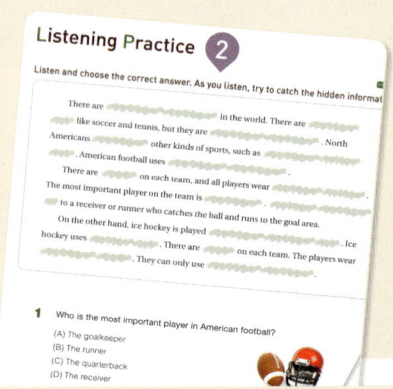

Listening Practice

다양한 내용의 청취 지문을 통해 본격적으로 청취 연습을 해본다.
① 중요 정보가 가려진 지문을 보면서 듣고 푸는 문제, ② 지문을 모두 듣고 푸는 문제 유형으로 연습되어진다.

*i*BT Practice

실제 토플 시험과 같은 상황을 제시하여 좀 더 긴 지문을 듣고 문제를 풀어본다. 각 장에서 연습한 실력을 최종적으로 점검하고 실전에 대비한다.

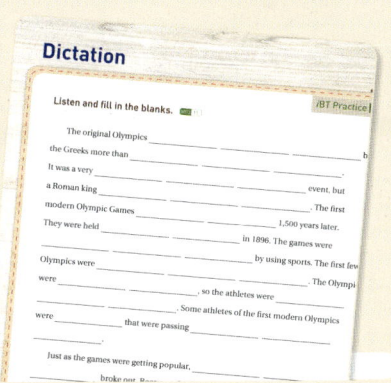

Dictation

받아쓰기는 청취력 향상을 위한 필수적인 연습 방법이다. *i*BT Practice에서 나온 지문을 다시 한번 듣고 받아 쓰는 연습을 통해 들리지 않고 이해되지 않았던 부분이 어디인지를 확인해본다.

Word Review

청취 능력뿐만 아니라 언어 능력 향상을 좌우하는 중요 요소 중의 하나인 어휘와 주요 표현을 정리한다. 각 장에서 사용되었던 중요 어휘와 표현을 문제를 통해 다시 한번 복습한다.

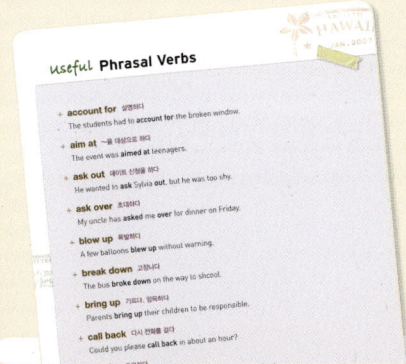

Useful Phrasal Verbs

문장을 이해하는데 가장 중요한 어휘력 향상을 위해 알아두면 유용한 phrasal verb의 의미를 예문을 통해 익힌다.

Contents

Chapter 1
Topic **History**   8
Question Type **Main Idea**

Overview	10
Basic Drills	12
Listening Practice	14
iBT Practice	20
Dictation	24
Word Review	26

Chapter 2
Topic **Sports**   28
Question Type **Supporting Detail**

Overview	30
Basic Drills	32
Listening Practice	34
iBT Practice	40
Dictation	44
Word Review	46

Chapter 3
Topic **Animals**   48
Question Type **Organization**

Overview	50
Basic Drills	52
Listening Practice	54
iBT Practice	60
Dictation	64
Word Review	66

Chapter 4
Topic **Plants**   68
Question Type **Organization-Rhetorical Connection**

Overview	70
Basic Drills	72
Listening Practice	74
iBT Practice	80
Dictation	84
Word Review	86

Chapter 5

Topic **Travel** 88
Question Type Content-Identifying Relationship

Overview	90
Basic Drills	92
Listening Practice	94
iBT Practice	100
Dictation	104
Word Review	106

Chapter 6

Topic **Food** 108
Question Type Content-Linking

Overview	110
Basic Drills	112
Listening Practice	114
iBT Practice	120
Dictation	124
Word Review	126

Chapter 7

Topic **Art & Entertainment** 128
Question Type Stance / Attitude

Overview	130
Basic Drills	132
Listening Practice	134
iBT Practice	140
Dictation	144
Word Review	146

Chapter 8

Topic **Social Issues** 148
Question Type Function-Purpose

Overview	150
Basic Drills	152
Listening Practice	154
iBT Practice	160
Dictation	164
Word Review	166

Mini Test 1-3 168

Scripts & Answer Key

Chapter 1
History

Topic:
History

Question Type:
Main Idea Questions
주제 찾기 문제
글의 전체적인 내용을 이해하는 문제

Main Idea Questions
주제 찾기 문제

1. 주제 찾기 문제는 들려주는 글의 전체적인 내용에 대한 것을 얼마나 이해하는 지를 묻는 유형의 문제이다.

2. 대화나 강의에 등장했던 여러 개의 소재들을 전반적으로 모두 포괄하는 주제를 찾도록 한다.

- What is the talk mainly about?
- What is the conversation mainly about?

Sample Question MP3 1

TOEFL Listening VOLUME HELP OK NEXT HIDE TIME 00:10:00

What is the talk mainly about?

Ⓐ The rules of basketball
Ⓑ The popularity of basketball
Ⓒ The birth of basketball
Ⓓ Basketball in the Olympics

Sctipt & 해석

Basketball is enjoyed by many people all over the world. The rules are simple, and people can either work as a team or play by themselves. Let's look at how the sport was born.

Dr. James Naismith worked in the YMCA in the US. He had to make a new game for people to play indoors when it was snowing or raining outside. He put two fruit baskets on top of poles and used a soccer ball. He made 13 simple rules, and the first game of basketball was played in 1891.

Basketball became popular very quickly. YMCAs all over the country had people playing basketball. Later, people replaced the baskets with hoops and nets. By 1936, it was introduced as an official event in the Berlin Olympics.

전세계 많은 이들이 농구를 즐긴다. 규칙이 간단하고 팀을 이루거나 혹은 혼자서도 경기를 할 수 있다. 농구가 어떻게 탄생했는지 살펴보자.

제임스 네스미쓰 박사는 미국 YMCA에서 일했다. 그는 눈이 오거나 비가 올 때 실내에서 사람들이 즐길 수 있는 새로운 게임을 만들어야 했다. 그는 두 개의 과일바구니를 막대 꼭대기에 달았고, 축구공을 이용했다. 그는 13개의 간단한 규칙을 만들었고, 최초의 농구 경기가 1891년에 있었다.

농구는 매우 급속히 대중화 되었다. 전국에 있는 YMCA는 사람들이 농구할 수 있게끔 했다. 후에 사람들은 바구니를 고리와 그물로 대체했다. 1936년에는 베를린 올림픽에 정식 종목으로 도입되었다.

Basic Drills 1

Listen and choose the correct answer. MP3 2-3

1 What is the conversation mainly about?

(A) Starting a war
(B) End of World War I
(C) End of World War II

🎧 Listen again and fill in the blanks.

> W: What's _____? You look worried.
> M: _____ _____ _____ I need to know when the Second World War was over.
> W: Really? Wasn't that in 1942? Wait, now I am confused. _____ _____ _____?
> M: No, I don't think so. I think it's _____ 1944 _____ 1945.

2 What is the talk about?

(A) Early postmen
(B) Horses
(C) Brave ponies

🎧 Listen again and fill in the blanks.

> The earliest postmen _____ _____ _____. The post offices were called the Pony Express. People would ride their horses _____ _____. There would be stations every 30 kilometers _____ _____ _____. Each rider rode for about 160 to 200 kilometers each time they made delivery. The brave riders rode their horses _____ _____ _____ the weather was like.

Basic Drills 2

Taking Notes: Symbols (I) - 기호

노트필기를 할때 문장을 그대로 받아적으려 하지 말고 기호 등을 사용하여 되도록 짧게 요약해서 적는다.

Mathematical Symbols

Symbol	Meaning	Example	Full Sentence
<	smaller, less important	my car < yours	My car is smaller than yours.
>	greater, more important	health > money	Health is more important than money.
=	is equal to, true	women = men	Women are equal to men.
≠	is not equal to, false	happiness ≠ money	Happiness is not about money.

On Your Own

1. Read the symbols and write the full sentence.

   (1) law = everyone

   _____

   (2) Kay's house > my uncle's

   _____

2. Listen and write the sentence using symbols. MP3 4

   (1) _____
   (2) _____

Listening Practice

Listen and choose the correct answer. As you listen, try to catch the hidden information.

~~~~~~~~~~ are very hard to learn. Long ago, Koreans ~~~~~~~~~~ as their written language. However, ~~~~~~~~~~. King Sejong realized that ~~~~~~~~~~ because common people ~~~~~~~~~~ the Chinese characters. ~~~~~~~~~~ knew how to read. King Sejong wanted ~~~~~~~~~~ a written language. He called the smartest scholars of Korea ~~~~~~~~~~ for Koreans.

After many years, King Sejong declared that ~~~~~~~~~~. Many Koreans were ~~~~~~~~~~. Hangul was ~~~~~~~~~~ than Chinese characters. King Sejong is still remembered today ~~~~~~~~~~.

1 What is the passage mainly about?

(A) People of Korea
(B) Writing in Chinese
(C) Life of King Sejong
(D) Birth of the Korean language

2 Why did King Sejong want to make a new language?

(A) Because people were lazy
(B) Because Chinese characters were hard to learn
(C) Because the King was bored
(D) Because Chinese characters were too easy

Listening Practice 2

Listen and choose the correct answer. As you listen, try to catch the hidden information.

The *Titanic* was ~~~~~~~~ in the world. It was also ~~~~~~~~. There were ~~~~~~~~ on the ship. The engineers were very sure ~~~~~~~~, so there were ~~~~~~~~.

Unfortunately, the *Titanic* ~~~~~~. The ship ~~~~~~~~ slowly. The lifeboats ~~~~~~~~ on the ship. Some lifeboats ~~~~~~ before they were full of passengers.

The people ~~~~~~~~ fell into the water. The water was very cold, and ~~~~~~~~. Other ships were ~~~~~~, so they could not ~~~~~~~~. Almost 1,500 people ~~~~~~~~.

1 What is the talk mainly about?

(A) The safety of the *Titanic*
(B) The sinking of the *Titanic*
(C) The passengers of the *Titanic*
(D) The engineers of the *Titanic*

2 Why did many people die?

(A) The people could not swim.
(B) There were many lifeboats.
(C) They froze to death.
(D) The ship was on fire.

Listening Practice 3

Listen and choose the correct answer.

Note-taking

1 What is the talk mainly about?

(A) The things Marco Polo did
(B) How merchants traveled
(C) Why Marco Polo traveled
(D) The way to be a merchant

2 According to the talk, what was China like during Marco Polo's time?

(A) China was very poor.
(B) China was very developed.
(C) China had many merchants.
(D) China had many ports.

Listening Practice 4

Listen and choose the correct answer.

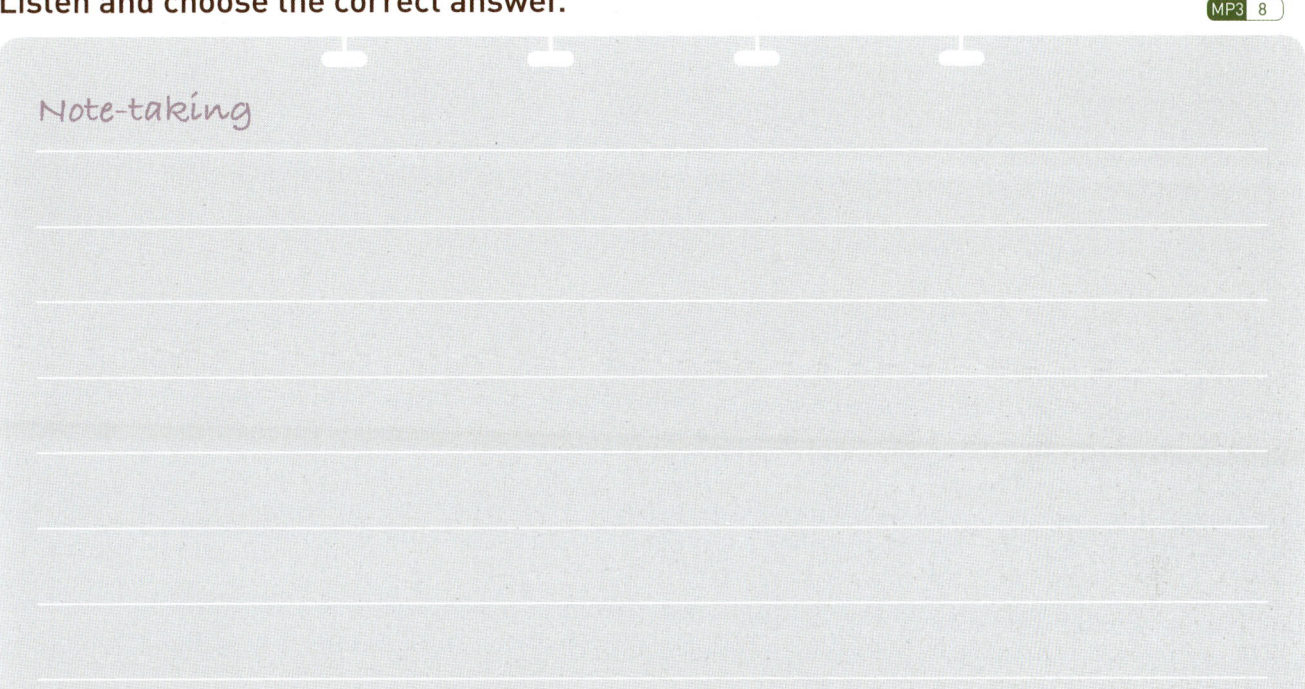

Note-taking

1 What is the discussion mainly about?

 (A) One black leader in America
 (B) Black Americans today
 (C) The Nobel Peace Prize
 (D) Two famous black leaders

2 What did Martin Luther King believe in?

 (A) He believed in Malcolm X.
 (B) He believed in fighting.
 (C) He believed in peaceful protests.
 (D) He believed in the Nobel Prize.

Listening Practice 5

Listen and choose the correct answer.

Note-taking

1 What is the talk mainly about?

   (A) Why men are better than women
   (B) Unfair treatment of women
   (C) Why women are better than men
   (D) Different clothes of men and women

2 What is one of the things women cannot do in some countries?

   (A) Driving cars
   (B) Making friends
   (C) Changing the law
   (D) Talking to people

Listening Practice 6

Listen and choose the correct answer.

MP3 10

Note-taking

1 What is the conversation mainly about?

(A) Getting rich with gold
(B) A wood factory made of gold
(C) The gold rush in Canada
(D) The gold rush in America

2 Why did many people suffer?

(A) They found gold on their journey.
(B) They were not prepared for the journey.
(C) They worked in a wood factory.
(D) They traveled to New York.

Chapter 1. History 19

iBT Practice 1

TOEFL Listening

1 What is the talk mainly about?

- Ⓐ The ancient Olympic Games
- Ⓑ The modern Olympic Games
- Ⓒ World Wars I and II
- Ⓓ Companies in the Olympic games

2 What does the speaker say about the first modern Olympics?

- Ⓐ They only had one event.
- Ⓑ They were very popular.
- Ⓒ They were on television.
- Ⓓ They were not very popular.

Note-taking

3 Who were the athletes of the first modern Olympics?

- Ⓐ All of the athletes were amateurs.
- Ⓑ All of the athletes were professionals.
- Ⓒ Some of the athletes were tourists.
- Ⓓ Some of the athletes were solders.

iBT Practice 2

TOEFL Listening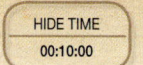

MP3 12

1 What is the talk mainly about?

- Ⓐ The roles of the Black Panthers
- Ⓑ The leaders of the Black Panthers
- Ⓒ The weapons of the Black Panthers
- Ⓓ The members of the Black Panthers

2 According to teacher, what did the Black Panthers do for black children?

- Ⓐ They gave dinner to black children every day.
- Ⓑ They gave lunch to black children every day.
- Ⓒ They gave breakfast to black children once.
- Ⓓ They gave breakfast to black children every day.

TOEFL Listening

Note-taking

3 Why did the Black Panthers train like soldiers?

Ⓐ They had nothing else to do.
Ⓑ They wanted to kill other people.
Ⓒ They wanted to protect themselves.
Ⓓ They werre better than other people.

Dictation

iBT Practice 1

Listen and fill in the blanks. MP3 11

The original Olympics _____ _____ _____ by the Greeks more than _____ _____ _____. It was a very _____ _____ _____ event, but a Roman king _____ _____ _____. The first modern Olympic Games _____ _____ 1,500 years later. They were held _____ _____ in 1896. The games were _____ _____ _____ by using sports. The first few Olympics were _____ _____ _____. The Olympics were _____ _____, so the athletes were _____ _____ _____. Some athletes of the first modern Olympics were _____ that were passing _____ _____ _____.

Just as the games were getting popular, _____ _____ _____ broke out. Because of this, the games _____ _____ _____. In fact, the modern games did not _____ _____ three times due to the World Wars.

Although the Olympics were not _____ _____, host countries _____ _____ _____ a lot of money. This was why big companies were allowed _____ _____ in the event. This made the Olympics a much _____ _____ than before.

iBT Practice 2

Listen and fill in the blanks. MP3 12

During the early 1900s, blacks in America _____ _____ _____ from white people. Blacks also had a very _____ _____ from the government. Because of this, two famous black Americans _____ _____ _____ called the Black Panthers.

The Black Panthers had guns and _____ _____ to fight like soldiers. They trained to _____ _____. They told black people _____ _____ _____ and fight. The Black Panthers also told other black Americans that _____ _____ _____ to white Americans. The government _____ _____ _____ the group, and they did not want black Americans _____ _____ _____.

The Black Panthers also helped _____ _____ _____. Most blacks during that time _____ _____, so they opened kitchens _____ _____ _____ to over 10,000 children every day. They also had newspapers _____ _____ _____ about the black community.

The government did many things to try and _____ _____ _____. For instance, they tried to make _____ _____ _____ by giving _____ _____ to other people. The government also had many famous _____ _____.

Chapter 1. History 25

Word Review

Match the words from the box with the definitions.

| replace | luxurious | sink | merchant |
| illegal | athlete | promote | feed |

1. _____ to go down under water
2. _____ not allowed by the law
3. _____ to put something in the place of another
4. _____ someone whose job is to buy and sell goods
5. _____ to give food to a person or an animal
6. _____ to help something to develop or increase
7. _____ very expensive, beautiful, and comfortable
8. _____ someone who does a sport, especially running, jumping, or throwing; someone who is good at sports

Choose the best phrase to fit in each one of the blanks.

| no matter what | broke out | takes place | suffered from |

9. He was only fifteen years old when the war _____.
10. Since the accident he has _____ headache and sleeplessness.
11. _____ happens, make sure that you mail that letter today.
12. The international film festival _____ every in April and lasts ten days.

useful **Phrasal Verbs**

+ **account for** 설명하다
  The students had to **account for** the broken window.

+ **aim at** ~을 대상으로 하다
  The event was **aimed at** teenagers.

+ **ask out** 데이트 신청을 하다
  He wanted to **ask** Sylvia **out**, but he was too shy.

+ **ask over** 초대하다
  My uncle has **asked** me **over** for dinner on Friday.

+ **blow up** 폭발하다
  A few balloons **blew up** without warning.

+ **break down** 고장나다
  The bus **broke down** on the way to shcool.

+ **bring up** 기르다, 양육하다
  Parents **bring up** their children to be responsible.

+ **call back** 다시 전화를 걸다
  Could you please **call back** in about an hour?

+ **call for** 요구하다
  The referee **called for** a doctor when the player got hurt.

+ **call off** 취소하다
  The game was **called off** because the rain did not stop.

+ **cheer up** 응원하다
  The good news **cheered** my famiily **up**.

Chapter 2
Sports

Topic:
Sports

Question Type:
Supporting Detail Questions
세부 사항 찾기 문제
글의 중요 세부 사항을 파악하는 문제

Supporting Detail Questions
세부 사항 찾기 문제

1. 세부 사항 찾기란 들려 주는 글의 주제와 관련되어 언급된 중요 세부 사항(important detail)에 대한 내용을 묻는 유형의 문제이다.

2. 청취 지문을 한번만 듣고 문제를 풀어야 하기 때문에 들려주는 대화나 글의 핵심 내용과 직접적으로 관련되지 않은 비교적 사소한 세부 사항(minor detail)은 보통 문제화되지 않는다.

3. 한 개 이상의 답을 요구하는 유형의 문제도 있다.

- According to the discussion, what is the meaning of sports?
- When was Pelé's final World Cup?

Sample Question MP3 13

TOEFL Listening

According to the talk, where is cricket NOT popular?

Ⓐ South Africa
Ⓑ North America
Ⓒ Britain
Ⓓ India

Sctipt & 해석

Bat and ball games are very popular in many countries. Baseball is even the national sport of some countries, such as the US, Japan, and Cuba. There is also a popular bat and ball game called cricket, which is slightly different from baseball.

Cricket is very popular with the British, Indians, and South Africans. Not many North Americans know about cricket. Cricket is played on a large circular field. Most of the game is played on a small rectangular area. It is different from the diamond-shaped field in baseball.

In baseball, there are 4 bases, and each base is about 28 meters away from each other. Cricket only has two bases, and they are 17 meters apart. The ball is thrown from about 20 meters, just like baseball. However, in cricket, the ball must bounce once on the ground before reaching the batter.

공과 막대기를 이용한 게임들은 많은 나라에서 인기가 있다. 야구는 미국, 일본, 쿠바 등의 나라에서는 국민 스포츠이다. 공과 막대기를 이용한 게임으로는 크리켓이라고 불리는 게임도 인기가 있는데 이 게임은 야구와 약간 다르다.

크리켓은 영국, 인도, 남아프리카 사람들 사이에서 인기가 있다. 북미 사람들 중에는 크리켓에 대해 아는 사람이 많지 않다. 크리켓은 커다랗고 둥근 경기장에서 행해지는데 경기는 주로 그 안에 있는 작은 직사각형에서 이루어진다. 야구의 다이아몬드 형 경기장과는 다르다.

야구에서는 네 개의 베이스가 있고 각각의 베이스는 서로 28미터씩 떨어져있다. 크리켓은 두 개의 베이스만 있고 17미터가 떨어져 있다. 공은 야구와 마찬가지로 20미터 밖에서 던져진다. 그러나 크리켓에서 공은 타자한테 가기 전에 바닥에 한번 튕겨져야 한다.

Basic Drills 1

Listen and choose the correct answer. MP3 14-15

1 Who trained with inline skates?

(A) Younger people
(B) Roller skaters
(C) Ice hockey players

🎧 Listen again and fill in the blanks.

> Many new sports _____ _____ _____ _____ every day. Some can become very popular. Inline skating is _____ _____ _____. It was used mainly _____ _____ _____ _____ who needed special skates to train in summer. The skates were very popular _____ _____ _____, and now, everyone likes inline skates.

2 Why do we need to exercise?

(A) To build stress
(B) To keep our minds healthy
(C) To make fewer friends

🎧 Listen again and fill in the blanks.

> W: Sports are _____ _____ _____. Everyone should play sports. Doctors say that we need the exercise _____ _____ our bodies healthy.
> M: Really? Is that _____ _____ _____ why we should play sports? I don't really care about health.
> W: Sports are also good _____ _____ _____ _____. They release stress, and you can also _____ _____ _____.

Basic Drills 2

Taking Notes: Symbols (II) - 기호

기호를 사용하여 노트필기를 할 때 자기만의 기호를 개발하여 활용해보자.

Identifying Cause & Effect

Symbol	Meaning	Example	Full Sentence
→	lead to, cause, mean	smoking → cancer	Smoking leads to cancer.
←	come from, because of	picnic canceled ← rain	The picnic was canceled because of rain.

On Your Own

1. Read the symbols and write the full sentence.

    (1) regular exercise → longer life
    _____

    (2) good manners ← good parenting
    _____

2. Listen and write the sentence using symbols. MP3 16

    (1) _____
    (2) _____

Listening Practice 1

Listen and choose the correct answer. As you listen, try to catch the hidden information.

All students in schools study hard and ~~~~~. Some even ~~~~~ ~~~~~. There are some students ~~~~~. ~~~~~, there are many schools that teach children ~~~~~ ~~~~~. The children study ~~~~~, but they must also ~~~~~ ~~~~~. The graduates of the schools are ~~~~~, and most become ~~~~~.

China is ~~~~~. This is because ~~~~~ start training ~~~~~. They eat and live ~~~~~. They study the same things in school like other students, but they also ~~~~~. They usually ~~~~~ than students in other schools.

1 What is the passage mainly about?

(A) Schools for normal children
(B) Schools for future athletes
(C) Schools for all students
(D) Schools for a better life

2 What do special school students in South America do after they graduate?

(A) The students stop playing soccer.
(B) The students go to diving schools.
(C) The students become soccer players.
(D) The students study in school again.

Listening Practice 2

MP3 18

Listen and choose the correct answer. As you listen, try to catch the hidden information.

There are ~~~~~~~~~~ in the world. There are ~~~~~~~~~~ ~~~~ like soccer and tennis, but they are ~~~~~~~~~~~~~. North Americans ~~~~~~~~ other kinds of sports, such as ~~~~~~~~ ~~~~~. American football uses ~~~~~~~~~~~~~~.

There are ~~~~~~ on each team, and all players wear ~~~~~~~~~~. The most important player on the team is ~~~~~~~ ~~~~~~~. ~~~ to a receiver or runner who catches the ball and runs to the goal area.

On the other hand, ice hockey is played ~~~~~~~~~~~~~~. Ice hockey uses ~~~~~~~~~. There are ~~~~~ on each team. The players wear ~~~~~~~~~~~~. They can only use ~~~~~~~~~~~.

1 Who is the most important player in American football?

(A) The goalkeeper
(B) The runner
(C) The quarterback
(D) The receiver

2 Which of the following are true of ice hockey?

	Yes	No
(A) They use a rugby ball.		
(B) The players wear protective clothes.		
(C) Players can only use their sticks.		
(D) There are 11 players on each team.		

Chapter 2. Sports 35

Listening Practice 3

Listen and choose the correct answer.

1 Who most often plays lacrosse in the US?

(A) Some old people
(B) High school and university students
(C) Everyone in the US
(D) Everyone in the world

2 How is lawn bowling played?

(A) Players roll balls on the grass.
(B) Players use sticks with nets.
(C) Players wear gloves and other gear.
(D) Players wait for the ball to move.

Listening Practice 4

Listen and choose the correct answer.

MP3 20

Note-taking

1 Who mainly watches the X Games?

(A) Young people all over the world
(B) Older people around the world
(C) Skaters and BMX riders
(D) Snowboarders and climbers

2 What is the main topic of the talk?

(A) ESPN
(B) Skaters and BMX riders
(C) Events for young people
(D) The X Games

Listening Practice 5

Listen and choose the correct answer.

MP3 21

Note-taking

1 How many players are on each curling team?

(A) 1 player
(B) 2 players
(C) 4 players
(D) 50 players

2 According to the talk, which is NOT true of the curling stone?

(A) It is round.
(B) It has triangular sides.
(C) It has a flat base.
(D) It has a handle on top.

Listening Practice 6

Listen and choose the correct answer.

MP3 22

Note-taking

---

1 Why did Ali change his name?

(A) He moved to the Middle East.
(B) He changed his boxing style.
(C) He changed to Islam.
(D) He wanted to be more famous.

2 Why did Ali refuse to join the war in Vietnam?

(A) He did not like the Vietnamese.
(B) He had no reason to fight.
(C) He wanted to box in the Olympics.
(D) He wanted to change his name to Ali.

iBT Practice 1

TOEFL Listening

1. What is the talk mainly about?

   A. How to rock climb in the mountains
   B. How rock climbing got dangerous
   C. How to use the equipment
   D. How rock climbing got popular

2. According to the man, what is one of the reasons rock climbing is getting safer?

   A. Many people read old information.
   B. Beginners practice climbing on indoor walls.
   C. Safety equipment is tested by elephants.
   D. Most climbing is done indoors.

Note-taking

3 How does the man talk about rock climbing?

(A) He gives examples of safety improvements in rock climbing.
(B) He compares the materials used to make indoor walls.
(C) He lists the companies that make climbing equipment.
(D) He describes how climbers change the way they climb.

*i*BT Practice 2

TOEFL Listening

1. According to the conversation, what new record did Korea make during the 2002 World Cup?

   A Watching television
   B Cheering in the streets
   C Playing in the World Cup
   D Winning the World Cup

2. Which country watched the 2002 World Cup the most on TV?

   A South Korea
   B Italy
   C Brazil
   D China

TOEFL Listening

Note-taking

3 According to the conversation, what are true of the 2002 World Cup? Tick in the correct box.

	Yes	No
Ⓐ FIFA claimed the 2002 World Cup as the most successful.		
Ⓑ The 2002 World Cup had teams from 100 countries.		
Ⓒ The 2002 World Cup had 25 days of games.		
Ⓓ Less than 25 millon people watched the 2002 World Cup.		

Dictation

iBT Practice 1

Listen and fill in the blanks. MP3 23

_____ _____ _____ have shown many people that _____ _____ can be fun and safe. _____ _____ is one of those sports. There are a few reasons why it is _____ _____ _____.

   Rock climbing is _____ _____ all the time. Companies are _____ _____ safer rock climbing gear. Long ago, _____ _____ _____ in rock climbing was of very _____ _____, and it was _____ _____ _____ to use it. These days, safety gear is _____ _____ to carry an elephant _____ _____.

   With better _____ _____, people have been able to develop _____ _____ _____ walls. This allows beginners _____ _____ _____, with proper coaching, _____ _____ _____. They can learn how to climb properly and be prepared _____ _____ _____ in the mountains.

   Rock climbing has also been viewed _____ _____ by many people due to old and _____ _____. The internet has helped people _____ _____ rock climbing. This has made _____ _____ _____ in the sport.

iBT Practice 2

Listen and fill in the blanks. MP3 24

W: So many people _____ _____ _____.
   I think it is the most _____ _____ on TV.

M: No, it's not. _____ _____ _____ is the most popular event.

W: Are you sure? There are more than _____ _____ that take part in the Olympics.

M: That is true. _____, _____ _____ watch the World Cup.

W: Wow, I didn't know that. _____ _____ _____ watch the World Cup?

M: It's different every time. In 2002, there were _____ _____ of games. In that time, _____ _____ _____ over 1 billion people watched the World Cup _____ _____. FIFA said that the 2002 World Cup was _____ _____ _____ World Cup so far.

W: That is a lot. Which country _____ _____ _____ watched the most?

M: In my opinion, China has _____ _____ _____, so they probably watched the most. During the World Cup, I think _____ _____ in the world watched the games. _____ _____ _____ watched the World Cup.

W: Oh, I heard that South Korea _____ _____ _____ for cheering outside _____ _____ _____. Over 4 million people watched the game between _____ _____ _____ in the streets. You know what? I was one _____ _____ _____!

Word Review

Match the words from the box with the definitions.

| protective | immediately | sweep | religion |
| jail | court | equipment | minimum |

1. _____ very quickly and without any delay
2. _____ used to keep someone or something safe from harm
3. _____ as small or little as possible
4. _____ a place where legal matters are decided by a judge and a jury
5. _____ to clean a floor, the ground, etc. using a brush with a long handle
6. _____ a place where people are kept as punishment for a crime
7. _____ the tools, machines, or other things that you need for a particular job or activity
8. _____ a particular system of belief in a god or gods, and all the activities that are related to it

Choose the best phrase to fit in each one of the blanks.

| refuses to | due to | take part in | an average of |

9. Teams from three different high schools will _____ the competition.
10. The poor harvest was _____ an unusually hot and dry summer.
11. _____ 3.4 traffic accidents per month occurs at this intersection.
12. No one trusts him, because he _____ take responsibility for his actions.

46 b-Listening

useful Phrasal Verbs

+ **call up** ~에게 전화하다
  We will **call up** Mr. Lawrence to ask about the assignment.

+ **carry on with** 계속하다
  Please **carry on with** what you were doing.

+ **carry out** ~을 이행하다
  The soldiers had to **carry out** the dangerous mission.

+ **catch up with** 따라잡다
  The policemen **caught up with** the robbers quickly.

+ **come about** 발생하다, 일어나다
  The French Revolution **came about** shortly after the American Revolution.

+ **come by** 들리다
  Uncle Dale will **come by** the house later to drop off our cousin, Victor.

+ **count on** 의지하다
  Can I **count on** you to wake me up tomorrow morning?

+ **cut out** 잘라내다
  The children **cut out** the paper to make stars.

+ **do over** 다시 하다
  We had to **do** our homework **over** because we did the wrong page.

+ **drop by** 예고 없이 방문하다
  We were surprised that Aunt Kate **dropped by** in the afternoon.

+ **dress up** 정장을 하다
  It's an informal potluck party, so you don't need to **dress up**.

Chapter 2. Sports **47**

Chapter 3
Animals

Topic:
Animals

Question Type:
Organization Questions
구성 인식 문제
글의 전체 구성을 파악하는 문제

Organization Questions
구성 인식 문제

1. 구성 인식 문제란 들려 주는 글의 전체 구성(organization)을 파악하는 능력을 확인하는 유형의 문제이다. 말하는 사람은 자신의 의견이나 정보를 효과적으로 전달하기 위하여 다양한 예(example), 열거(list), 비교(comparison), 대조(contrast), 또는 시간 순서(time order) 등의 다양한 구성 방식을 활용할 수 있다는 것을 알아 두자.

2. 글의 구성을 파악하기 위해서는 다음과 같은 표현에 유의한다.
   - 예시(example): for example, for instance
   - 분류(classification): next, first, second
   - 대조(contrast): on the other hand, unlike, however
   - 시간 순서(chronological, time order): by the time, later
   - 원인과 결과(cause and effect): as a result, therefore, due to

- How does the speaker talk about dinosaurs and humans?
- In what order does the speaker talk about blue whales?

Sample Question MP3 25

TOEFL Listening

How does the speaker talk about camels living in the desert?

Ⓐ She mentions the way camels walk.
Ⓑ She contrasts camels with other animals.
Ⓒ She gives examples of other deserts.
Ⓓ She describes camels controlling their body.

Sctipt & 해석

There are very few animals in the desert, because it is very hot and there is very little water or food. One animal that can live in the desert is the camel.

Camels need very little water, and they can control their body temperature easily. Controlling body temperature means that they sweat very little, even in the desert. This is why camels can walk a very long time without water.

The humps of camels are where energy is stored, not water. They use the energy stored in the humps when there is no food to eat. As a result, camels do not need to be fed all the time when crossing the desert.

사막은 아주 덥고 물도 먹이도 부족하기 때문에 동물들이 거의 살지 않는다. 사막에서 살수 있는 동물로 낙타를 들 수 있다.

낙타는 물을 거의 필요로 하지 않고 체온을 쉽게 조절한다. 체온을 조절한다는 것은 사막에서도 땀을 거의 흘리지 않는다는 것을 의미한다. 이것이 바로 낙타가 물 없이 먼 길을 걸어갈 수 있는 이유이다.

낙타의 등에 있는 혹은 물이 아닌 에너지의 저장고이다. 낙타는 먹을 것이 없을 때 혹에 저장해 놓은 에너지를 소비한다. 그 결과 낙타는 사막을 건너는 동안에 항상 먹이를 줄 필요가 없다.

Basic Drills 1

Listen and choose the correct answer. MP3 26-27

1 In what order does the speaker talk about kangaroos raising babies?

(A) From leaving the pouch to birth
(B) From birth to playing outside of the pouch
(C) From birth to leaving the pouch completely

🎧 Listen again and fill in the blanks.

> Kangaroos have _____ _____ _____ of raising babies. The mother _____ _____ to a 2.5 cm baby. The baby stays in the mother's pouch and drinks milk. When the baby is _____ _____ _____, it starts to play outside of the mother's pouch. When the baby is ten months old, the baby _____ _____ _____ completely.

2 How does the speaker talk about blue whales?

(A) By comparing size with dinosaurs
(B) By mentioning the weight of the whales
(C) By giving examples of larger animals

🎧 Listen again and fill in the blanks.

> M: What is the largest animal _____ _____ _____ on earth?
> W: That's easy. It's the blue whale.
> M: Are you serious? I thought _____ _____ _____ _____ a dinosaur.
> W: No, the blue whale is _____ _____ any dinosaur.
> M: How about the smallest?
> W: _____ _____ _____ would have to be an amoeba.

Basic Drills 2

Taking Notes: Abbreviations (I) - 약어, 축약형

영어의 단어를 그대로 적기보다는 단어의 철자를 줄여 일부만을 적으면 노트필기를 할 때 시간 절약뿐 아니라 간단히 필기하는데 도움이 된다.

Abbreviation	co.	diff.	w/	w/o
Meaning	company	difficult	with	without

On Your Own

1. Read the abbreviations and write out the full word.

    (1) jr. – _____   (2) Q. – _____

    (3) e.g. – _____   (4) 2nd – _____

2. Try to make your own abbreviations

    (1) answer – _____   (2) benefit – _____

    (3) number – _____   (4) newspaper – _____

3. Listen and write the sentence using symbols and abbreviations. MP3 28

    (1) _____

    (2) _____

Chapter 3. Animals

Listening Practice

Listen and choose the correct answer. As you listen, try to catch the hidden information.

There are many animals on earth. Some animals are very big, and some are very small. Humans are animals, too, but we are ~~~~~~~~~~~~ ~~~~~~.

We are the only animals in the world ~~~~~~~~~~. No other animal ~~~ ~~~~~~~~~~ for a long time. Animals need ~~~~~~~~~~~~~~, and to jump. ~~~~~~~~~~~~~~~~~~~~~~~ from other animals. Because of this, only humans ~~~~~~~~~~, and all other animals ~~~~~~~~~~.

~~~~~~~~, humans are one of the few animals in the world ~~~~~~~~. Scientists think that ~~~~~~~~~~~~, but ~~~~~~~~~~~~~~~~. However, most other animals, ~~~~~~~~~~, ~~~~~~~~. Their tails are used ~~~~~~~~~~~~~~~~~.

1 What is the cheetah's tail used for?

(A) The tail is used to sleep lying down.
(B) The tail does not have any use.
(C) The tail is used to balance.
(D) The tail is used to jump.

2 How does the speaker explain the difference between humans and animals?

(A) He compares running style.
(B) He compares bone design.
(C) He talks about animals without tails.
(D) He gives examples of cheetahs.

Listening Practice 2

Listen and choose the correct answer. As you listen, try to catch the hidden information.

M: Hi, Sylvia. ~~~~~~~~~?

W: I've got ~~~~~~~~ today. I am taking ~~~~~~~~ in the afternoon.

M: Why? Is there ~~~~~~~~~~?

W: No, he is ~~~~~~~. I always get him ~~~~~~~~~~~.

M: How often do you ~~~~~~~~~?

W: I ~~~~~~~~~ every six months. Just to be sure, I also ~~~~~~~~ ~~~~~~~. If I don't give my dog that medicine, he can ~~~~~~~.

M: Oh, that would be terrible. It sounds like ~~~~~~~~~ to keep dogs healthy. Is there ~~~~~~?

W: I also ~~~~~~~~~ every day. That way, both he and I ~~~~~~~~. That's how owners ~~~~~~~~~ properly.

1 What is the talk mainly about?

(A) Exercising with dogs
(B) Going for a checkup
(C) Taking care of dogs properly
(D) What to do when dogs are sick

2 How does the woman talk about taking care of dogs?

(A) She contrasts different types of dogs.
(B) She talks of her personal experience.
(C) She lists the benefits of pets.
(D) She mentions the different types of medicine.

Listening Practice 3

Listen and choose the correct answer.

MP3 31

Note-taking

---

1 Which of the following are true about blue whales? Tick in the correct box.

	Yes	No
(A) Blue whales are as big as elephants.		
(B) Baby whales are 2 tons at birth.		
(C) Adult blue whales eat about 80 kg of food every day.		
(D) Adult blue whales weigh 130 tons.		

2 In what order does the speaker talk about blue whales?

(A) From eating to drinking milk
(B) From adult whales to baby whales
(C) From hunting to fighting off enemies
(D) From birth to adult whales

Listening Practice 4

Listen and choose the correct answer.

MP3 32

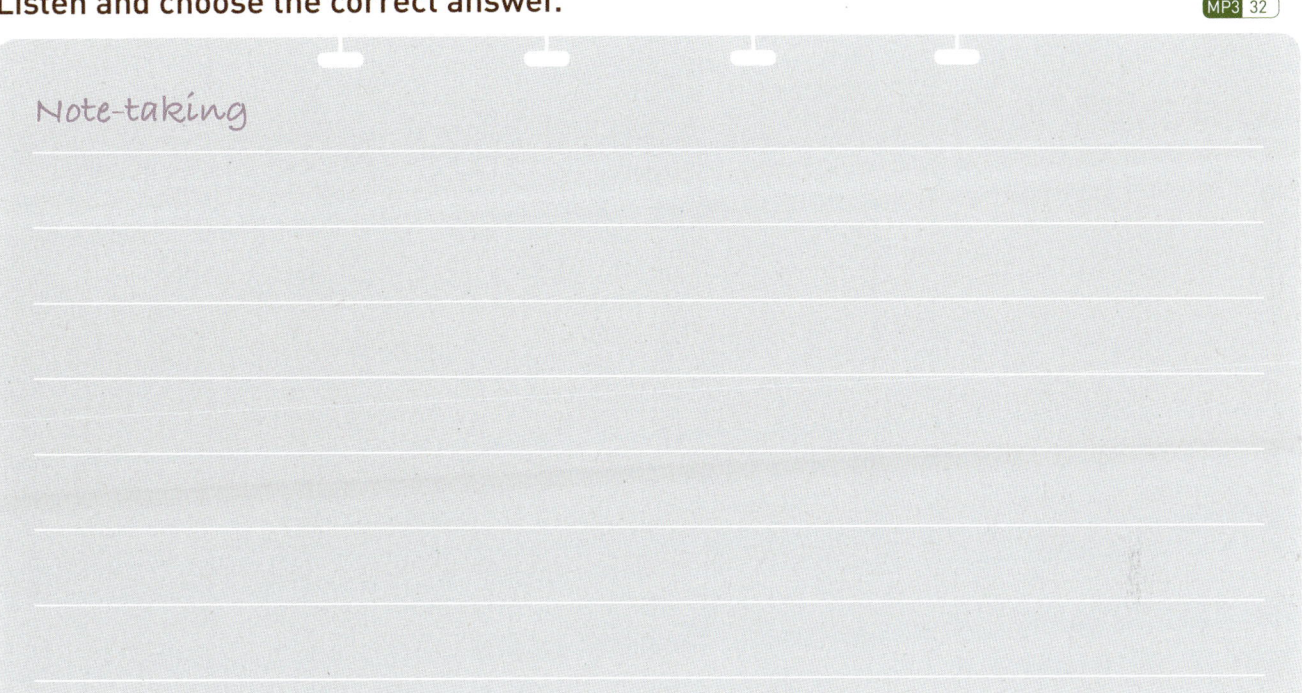

Note-taking

1 How does the man stress the importance of Dian Fossey's work?

(A) By giving examples of all the animals that have disappeared
(B) By mentioning different types of gorillas
(C) By giving his personal experience in Africa
(D) By mentioning the Gorilla Fund International

2 What is the conversation mainly about?

(A) The work of Dian Fossey
(B) The gorillas in Africa
(C) The killer of Dian Fossey
(D) The gorillas in the mountains

Listening Practice 5

Listen and choose the correct answer.

Note-taking

1 According to the talk, how long does the sloth sleep?

(A) The sloth sleeps for 20 hours a day.
(B) The sloth sleeps for 8 days.
(C) The sloth sleeps for 8 hours every day.
(D) The sloth hardly sleeps at all.

2 How does the speaker stress that the sloth is a lazy animal?

(A) He mentions that the sloth sleeps very little.
(B) He gives examples of the sloth's lifestyle.
(C) He talks about the trees that the sloth lives in.
(D) He compares the sloth to turtles.

Listening Practice 6

Listen and choose the correct answer.

1 How can owners of fish get better health from their pets?

(A) By making them exercise
(B) By looking at them to reduce stress
(C) By carrying diseases inside them
(D) By making the fish fetch a ball and bark

2 How does the teacher talk about pets and humans?

(A) By listing the benefits of having pets
(B) By giving examples of how pets exercise
(C) By contrasting different animals
(D) By mentioning fur and diseases

Chapter 3. Animals 59

*i*BT Practice 1

TOEFL Listening

1 How does the teacher talk about night animals?

- Ⓐ He gives examples of two night animals.
- Ⓑ He lists the mice that come out at night.
- Ⓒ He explains all the senses used by animals.
- Ⓓ He compares which sense is more useful.

2 How do bats look for food at night?

- Ⓐ By flying around and looking for food
- Ⓑ By looking at the source of sounds
- Ⓒ By making noise and listening to echoes
- Ⓓ By looking only left and right

TOEFL Listening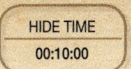

Note-taking

3 According to the teacher, where are the ears of owls?

Ⓐ They are on the wings.
Ⓑ They are on top of the head.
Ⓒ They are on the body.
Ⓓ They are on the face.

iBT Practice 2

TOEFL Listening

1. What is the conversation mainly about?

   A. Different names of humans
   B. Different names of large animals
   C. Different names of male, female and baby animals
   D. Different names of cows and bulls

2. How does the man talk about the names of large animals?

   A. He gives examples of animals with the same name.
   B. He explains what large animals are.
   C. He compares different types of kangaroos.
   D. He lists all the animals with different names.

TOEFL Listening

Note-taking

3 According to the conversation, which of the following are true about the names of animals? Tick in the correct box.

	Yes	No
Ⓐ Baby chickens are called roosters.		
Ⓑ Male crocodiles are called bulls.		
Ⓒ Female cats are called tomcats.		
Ⓓ Baby kangaroos are called joeys.		

Dictation

iBT Practice 1

Listen and fill in the blanks. MP3 35

Most animals have _____ _____ _____, because they are active _____ _____ _____. However, night animals are a little bit different. They are animals that become _____ _____ _____. These animals use _____ _____, such as hearing, taste or _____ _____ _____ at night.

For example, bats _____ _____, but they do not use them. _____, they see by using _____ _____. They _____ _____ and listen to the echoes _____ _____ _____. This tells them what is _____ _____ _____, and what is _____ _____. It is a very effective way of _____ _____. In fact, it is so effective that _____ _____ have used this method _____ " _____ " _____.

Owls use both _____ and sound to hunt for food. They have very _____ _____, and they can only see _____ _____. Owls must _____ _____ _____ to see left and right. This is because the owls' sensitive ears are _____ _____ _____. Since their eyes do not move, they find _____ _____ of mice easily by simply looking at where the sound _____ _____ _____. The owl can also hear sounds from very _____ _____.

iBT Practice 2

Listen and fill in the blanks. MP3 36

W: There are so many _____ _____ to learn!

M: If you think there are _____ _____, you should also know that there are _____ _____ for male, female and _____ _____, too.

W: What do you mean?

M: I'm sure _____ _____ _____ of a male chicken being called _____ _____ and a female chicken _____ _____.

W: Yes, that much I know, but do all animals have _____ _____ for males and females?

M: Most animals _____ _____ _____. Some animals share _____ _____ _____, too. Males _____ _____ _____ are called bulls, and females are called _____. Their baby is called _____ _____.

W: Aren't they the names _____ _____?

M: Yes, you are right. But _____ _____ the animal is not a cow, _____ _____ a crocodile or a whale, they are still called _____ _____ _____.

W: That is _____. I didn't know any of that.

M: Also, _____ _____ are tomcats, females are _____, and babies are _____. I'll tell you one more. _____ _____ are called jacks, and female kangaroos are called _____. Baby kangaroos are called _____.

W: Wow, there seems to be so much that I still _____ _____ _____.

Chapter 3. Animals **65**

Word Review

Match the words from the box with the definitions.

| temperature | sweat | pouch | vet |
| tragic | insect | echo | object |

1. _____ extremely sad, because someone suffers or dies
2. _____ a solid thing that you can see and touch, but that is not alive
3. _____ the degree of how hot or cold a place or thing is
4. _____ a doctor for animals
5. _____ a pocket of skin in which a certain kind of animal such as a kangaroo carries its baby
6. _____ to have drops on your skin because you are hot, ill, or doing exercise
7. _____ a small creature such as a fly or ant, that has six legs, and sometimes wings
8. _____ a sound that is repeated because it hits something such as a wall and returns

Choose the best phrase to fit in each one of the blanks.

| gave birth to | take care of | bounce off | straight ahead |

9. Look _____, and do not look to the right or left.
10. When sound waves _____ an object and return, we hear an echo.
11. We offered to _____ their dog while they were out of town.
12. She _____ a healthy baby boy at 1:30 p.m. yesterday.

useful Phrasal Verbs

+ **eat out** 외식하다

There's nothing in the refrigerator. Why don't we **eat out**?

+ **eat away** 서서히 파괴하다

The metal boat was **eaten away** by the sea.

+ **figure out** 알아내다

We had to **figure out** a way to get the dog out of the hole.

+ **fill in** 대신하다

Mr. Lynch **filled in** for the sick math teacher.

+ **fill out** 작성하다

We have to **fill out** some forms before we can buy a mobile phone.

+ **fill up** 채우다

The students **filled up** the tank for the fish to swim in.

+ **find out** 알게 되다

It was a pleasant surprise to **find out** that she had won the contest.

+ **get along** 사이 좋게 지내다

Please do not argue. Why don't you two **get along** with each other?

+ **get at** ~이르다, 닿다

The child tried to **get at** the cookie jar, but he was too short.

+ **get away** 달아나다

Sometimes I wish to **get away** from everything and relax in a quiet place.

+ **get in** 도착하다

The plane **gets in** at 3 p.m. local time.

Chapter 4
Plants

Topic:
Plants

Question Type:
Organization-Rhetorical Connection Questions
수사학적 구성 인식 문제
특정 내용과 글의 전체 구성의 관계를 파악하는 문제

Organization-Rhetorical Connection Questions
수사학적 구성 인식 문제

1. 말하는 이가 자신의 생각이나 말하고자 하는 내용을 효과적으로 전달하기 위해서 사용하는 표현 방식을 수사학(rhetoric)이라고 한다.

2. 수사학적 구성 인식 문제는 화자(speaker)가 언급한 특정 내용(a particular statement)이 전체적인 글의 구성에서 수사학적으로(rhetorically) 어떻게 관련되어 있는지를 묻는 유형의 문제이다. 다음과 같은 요소를 확인할 수 있는 능력을 평가한다.
   - 화제 전환(topic shift)의 형태
   - 예증(exemplification)의 형태
   - 주제에서 살짝 옆으로 빗나가 다른 얘기를 하는 지엽(digressions)의 형태
   - 머리말(introduction)이나 맺음말(concluding)의 형태

   - Why does the teacher mention lions and tigers?
   - Why does the woman mention seaweed?

Sample Question MP3 37

TOEFL Listening

Why does the teacher mention Mexico and the US?

Ⓐ To compare the amount of rain in each country
Ⓑ To talk about all the plants in Mexico and the US
Ⓒ To give information about where cactus plants live
Ⓓ To emphasize the deserts of the two countries

Sctipt & 해석

There are many types of cactus plants in the deserts of Mexico and the US. Most cactus plants have sharp needles, which are actually the plant leaves. There are two reasons why cactus leaves are so sharp.

First, the sharp leaves make it very hard for animals to reach the water in the cactus. This is important because the cactus plant is one of the only things in the desert that hold a lot of water. Therefore, the cactus plant needs to protect itself from the animals that want the water.

Second, the cactus plant also has very thin leaves to slow down water from drying up. Having thin leaves means that the plant cannot make a lot of energy, but can save a lot of water. As there is very little rain or water in the desert, thin leaves are necessary to cactus plants.

멕시코나 미국에 있는 사막에서는 많은 종류의 선인장을 볼 수 있다. 많은 선인장들은 뾰족한 가시들을 갖고 있는데, 이 가시들은 실제로 선인장의 잎들이다. 선인장의 잎이 왜 뾰족한 지에는 두 가지 이유가 있다.

첫째는, 뾰족한 잎들은 선인장 안에 있는 물을 동물들이 가질 수 없게 만든다. 선인장은 사막에 있는 많은 양의 물을 저장할 수 있는 몇 안 되는 식물 중 하나이기 때문에 매우 중요한 사실이다. 그러므로 선인장은 물을 원하는 동물들로부터 자신들을 보호할 필요가 있는 것이다.

둘째는, 선인장의 뾰족한 잎은 또한 선인장의 수분 증발 속도를 늦춘다. 뾰족한 잎을 가졌다는 것은 이 식물이 많은 에너지를 만들 수는 없지만, 많은 물을 저장할 수 있다는 것을 의미한다. 사막에는 비나 물이 거의 없기 때문에 뾰족한 잎은 선인장에 꼭 필요하다.

Basic Drills 1

Listen and choose the correct answer. MP3 38-39

1 Why does the speaker mention oranges?

(A) To list all the minerals in fruits
(B) To compare vitamins in vegetables
(C) To give an example of a fruit with vitamins

🎧 Listen again and fill in the blanks.

> Humans cannot live on this earth _____ _____ _____. Doctors say that we must eat a lot of vegetables to have _____ _____ _____ because they contain minerals and fiber. Fruits are also plants. We get most of our vitamins and sugar _____ _____. Fruits, such as oranges, have _____ _____ vitamin C.

2 Why does the speaker mention that there are many types of fruits in the world?

(A) To introduce fruits as a topic
(B) To give examples of plants
(C) To start naming all the fruits of the world

🎧 Listen again and fill in the blanks.

> There are _____ _____ of fruits in this world. However, no country can grow all the fruits of the world _____ _____. The weather is important to grow fruits. For instance, _____ _____ _____, there are a lot of mangoes and melons. _____ _____ _____, there are many strawberries and apples.

Basic Drills 2

Taking Notes: Abbreviations (II) - 약어, 축약형

약어를 사용하여 노트필기를 할 때, 글자를 많이 줄이면 나중에 어떤 단어를 쓴 건지 구분할 수 없게 되므로 주의한다. 보통 첫음절 이후에는 모음을 생략하여 약어를 만든다.

Abbreviation	M.J.	comm.	govt.	envirnmnt.
Meaning	Michael Jackson	communication	government	environment

On Your Own

1. Read the abbreviations and write out what you think is the correct word.

   (1) dept. – _____   (2) imp. – _____
   (3) lang. – _____   (4) info. – _____

2. Make abbreviations of the following words.

   (1) problems – _____   (2) transportation – _____
   (3) elevator – _____   (4) maximum – _____

3. Listen and write the sentence using symbols and abbreviations. [MP3 40]

   (1) _____
   (2) _____

Listening Practice 1

Listen and choose the correct answer. As you listen, try to catch the hidden information.

When we get sick, we take medicine. ~~~~~~~~~~~~~~ that can fight off sickness and make us feel better. ~~~~~~~~~~~~~~ ~~~~.

Plants are a very important part ~~~~~~~~~~~~~~. Plants used in traditional medicine ~~~~~~~~~~~~. Many different types of herbs ~~~~~~~~~~~~~~. Some herbs ~~~~~~~~~~, or they ~~~~~~~~~~.

Plants also play a very important part ~~~~~~~~~~~~. More and more plants are used ~~~~~~~~~~~~~~. Medicine companies are always trying ~~~~~~~~~~~~~~. In fact, scientists are now trying ~~~~~~~~~~~~~~ ~~~~~~~~~~~ as only 5% of sea plants have been tested so far.

1 How does the teacher talk about plants as medicine?

(A) He compares which medicine is better.
(B) He mentions plants in traditional and modern medicine.
(C) He lists the plants that are used as medicine.
(D) He gives reasons why herbs are used as medicine.

2 Why does the teacher mention that different things are mixed to make medicine?

(A) To introduce plants being used as medicine
(B) To compare different things in medicine
(C) To list all the things in medicine
(D) To encourage the students to talk about medicine

Listening Practice 2

Listen and choose the correct answer. As you listen, try to catch the hidden information.

W: Did you know that there are ~~~~~~?

M: I know fish live in the sea, ~~~~~~~~~? I have not heard of such a thing.

W: ~~~~~~~~~~~, but that's only one type. In fact, ~~~~~~~~~~~~~~~~~~~~~~~~~~~~~~~~.

M: What? Now you're really joking. Everyone knows that ~~~~~~~~~~~~~~.

W: Yes, plants on land ~~~~~~~~~~~~~~. There are a lot of very small plants ~~~~~~~~~~~~~~~~~~~~~~~~~~~~. These plants ~~~~~~~~~~~~~~~~~~~~~~~~~~~~~~~ in the world.

M: Wow, I didn't know that. We should ~~~~~~~~~~~~~~~~~~. I don't want the ocean ~~~~~~~~~~~~~.

W: Yes, that is an important reason ~~~~~~~~~~~~.

1 What is the talk mainly about?

(A) Sea animals giving out oxygen
(B) Sea animals in the ocean
(C) Sea plants in the ocean
(D) Trees floating in the sea

2 Why does the woman mention seaweed?

(A) To describe sea plants making oxygen
(B) To give an example of a sea plant
(C) To list all the different sea plants
(D) To mention trees giving out oxygen

Listening Practice 3

Listen and choose the correct answer.

MP3 43

Note-taking

1 What is the conversation mainly about?

(A) Food of big animals
(B) Food of small animals
(C) The food chain process
(D) Lunch in the playground

2 Why does the woman mention fruits and nuts?

(A) To give an example of food for small animals
(B) To compare with the food chain process
(C) To introduce a new topic in the discussion
(D) To find out if the man knows about it

Listening Practice 4

Listen and choose the correct answer.

Note-taking

1 What is the talk mainly about?

(A) The characteristics of bamboo
(B) The uses of fast growing trees
(C) The different homes in Bangladesh
(D) The reasons for bamboo growth

2 Why does the woman mention trees taking 60 years to grow 20 meters?

(A) To list examples of fast growing things
(B) To explain how the tree are used
(C) To stress how quickly bamboo can grow
(D) To show that bamboo can grow very slowly

Listening Practice 5

Listen and choose the correct answer.

Note-taking

1. What is the conversation mainly about?

   (A) Using plants to make rags
   (B) Paper made from different plants
   (C) Drawing on different paper
   (D) Egyptian paper

2. Why does the woman mention that rags were also used to make paper?

   (A) To give another example of paper not made from wood
   (B) To emphasize that the Chinese were the first to make paper
   (C) To show which paper is better
   (D) To change the topic of the conversatio

Listening Practice 6

Listen and choose the correct answer.

MP3 46

Note-taking

---

1 Why does the speaker mention plants not having a brain?

(A) To explain how plants think
(B) To give examples of different plants around the world
(C) To show that animals are smarter than plants
(D) To introduce the difference between plants and animals

2 According to the talk, what do plants have in cells?

(A) They have brain cells.
(B) They have cell walls.
(C) They have oxygen cells.
(D) They have muscle cells.

iBT Practice 1

TOEFL Listening

1 What is the talk mainly about?

- Ⓐ Plants that eat other plants
- Ⓑ Plants that eat meat
- Ⓒ Animals that eat plants
- Ⓓ Animals that eat meat

2 Why does the teacher mention lions and tigers?

- Ⓐ To begin talking about lions and tigers
- Ⓑ To give examples of where carnivores live
- Ⓒ To point out that only animals are called carnivores
- Ⓓ To provide background information about carnivores

Note-taking

3 Which of the following are true of carnivorous plants?
Tick in the correct box.

	Yes	No
Ⓐ They eat meat.		
Ⓑ They chew the insect.		
Ⓒ They eat other plants.		
Ⓓ They use smell to attract insects.		

iBT Practice 2

1 What are the students discussing?

- Ⓐ Trees with mushrooms
- Ⓑ Hunting with pigs and dogs
- Ⓒ The most expensive food in the world
- Ⓓ Different food grown in Europe

2 Why does the woman mention the taste of truffles?

- Ⓐ To find out more about truffles
- Ⓑ To contrast with other mushrooms
- Ⓒ To state more characteristics of truffles
- Ⓓ To test the man's knowledge about truffles

TOEFL Listening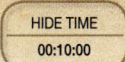

Note-taking

3 What are the reasons truffles are so expensive?
Tick in 2 answers.

Ⓐ Truffles have a strong smell.
Ⓑ Truffles are hard to find.
Ⓒ Truffles take a long time to grow.
Ⓓ Truffles are made by pigs and dogs.

Dictation

iBT Practice 1

Listen and fill in the blanks. MP3 47

    Carnivores are animals that _____ _____ _____ their whole lives, such as _____ _____ _____.
Many animals in the world are carnivores. Strangely, there are _____ _____ that are also carnivores because they _____ _____.
_____ _____ _____ is a well-known carnivore.
The Venus flytrap has a large trap to _____ _____.
The flies _____ _____ _____ and think that _____ _____ _____. When the fly lands on the area, the legs _____ _____ on the plant. The plant _____ _____ _____ and slowly eats the fly _____ _____ _____.

    Another carnivorous plant is _____ _____ _____.
The flower of the plant looks like a funny _____ _____. It hangs on the end of _____ _____ _____. The pitcher plant also _____ _____ by smell. The bottom of the pitcher contains a powerful _____ _____ _____ insects for food. Ants and other _____ _____ think that there is a lot of food _____ _____ _____. The insect will try to _____ _____ _____ inside the pitcher. The sides of the pitcher walls are _____ _____, and the insect falls _____ _____ _____ of the pitcher.

84 b-Listening

iBT Practice 2

Listen and fill in the blanks. MP3 48

M: My teacher told us _____ _____ _____ about the most _____ _____ in the world. Could you tell me _____ _____ _____?

W: Well, some people say that _____ _____ is the most expensive. It is _____ _____, and there are _____ _____ of truffles. The most expensive truffles grow _____ _____ _____.

M: Mushrooms? _____ _____ _____?

W: No, I'm not. Truffles _____ _____ _____ of pine trees. Naturally, truffles _____ _____. That is why it is very hard for people _____ _____ _____.

M: Then how do _____ _____ find these mushrooms?

W: _____ _____ or dogs find truffles _____ _____. They are the only animals that people use _____ _____ _____. Truffles are also expensive because they take a very long _____ _____ _____.

M: Well, how expensive are _____ _____ _____? After all, it's only a mushroom.

W: _____ _____ truffle prices that I have heard of are _____ _____ _____ for 1 kilogram.

M: What! That's so expensive! Just how _____ _____ _____ truffles?

W: People cut them into very _____ _____ and serve them together _____ _____ or other types of food _____ _____. I'll tell you about the taste of truffles when we _____ _____ _____. I'm going home now.

Word Review

Match the words from the box with the definitions.

| climate | oxygen | float | cell |
| absorb | trap | melt | attract |

1 _____ the smallest part of a living structure

2 _____ the typical weather conditions in a particular area

3 _____ to change something solid into a liquid

4 _____ to take in a gas, liquid, or other substances

5 _____ something designed or used for catching animals

6 _____ to stay the surface of a liquid without sinking

7 _____ to make people interested in something so that they come to it

8 _____ a gas in the air that has no color or smell, and is necessary for most animals to live

Choose the best phrase to fit in each one of the blanks.

| plenty of | at once | are made of | instead of |

9 There is _____ time to finish your meal, so please do not hurry.

10 I wrote down her name as "Coral" _____ "Carol" by mistake.

11 When you hear the alarm bell ring, leave the building _____.

12 Some buildings _____ such strong materials that they last hundreds of years.

useful **Phrasal Verbs**

+ **get on** 올라타다
  Hurry up and **get on** the bus before it leaves.

+ **get off** 내리다
  Peter will **get off** at the next station.

+ **get over** 극복하다
  It was hard for me to **get over** the operation.

+ **get through** 통과하다, 끝내다
  Susan had a lot of homework, but she **got through** it all by 10.

+ **give away** 나누어주다
  The singer **gave away** her CDs to her fans on stage.

+ **give back** 돌려주다
  Tony found a wallet in the street and tried to **give** it **back** to the owner.

+ **give up** 항복하다
  The robbers **gave up** because they could not escape.

+ **go ahead** 계속하다
  We had to **go ahead** to summer camp without Mrs. Lopez.

+ **go on** 계속하다
  He insisted that they should **go on** with the project.

+ **go up** 오르다
  The price of pizza has gone up by 2 dollars.

+ **hand in** 제출하다
  The teacher wanted us to **hand in** our homework before he left.

Chapter 4. Plants 87

Chapter 5
Travel

Topic:
Travel

Question Type:
Content-Identifying
Relationship Questions
내용 관계 확인 문제
언급된 사항들간의 관계를 파악하는 문제

Content-Identifying Relationship Questions

내용 관계 확인 문제

1. 내용 관계 확인 문제란 들려주는 전체 글 중에서 분명하게 언급(clearly stated)된 내용간의 관계에 대해 확인하는 유형의 문제이다.

2. 예를 들어, 원인과 결과로서 무엇이 언급되었는지, 내용의 진행이 어떤 순서로 기술되었는지, 또는 언급된 사실이 어떠한 내용으로 비교가 되었는지 등에 대해 물어본다.

- What is compared between the Ganges and other rivers around the world?
- What comparison is made between Seoul and Busan?
- What was the result of the Renaissance?

Sample Question MP3 49

TOEFL Listening VOLUME HELP OK NEXT HIDE TIME 00:10:00

What is compared between the Channel Tunnel and the Seikan Tunnel?

Ⓐ The location of the tunnel
Ⓑ The length of the tunnel
Ⓒ The trains in the tunnel
Ⓓ The number of tunnels

Sctipt & 해석

The first person to try digging a tunnel between England and France was Napoleon. However, it took too much time. Then, in 1994, a 50-km-long tunnel called the Channel Tunnel was finally completed and joined the two countries together.

It took over 15,000 workers and over 7 years to finish digging the tunnel. The dirt that was dug out was used to make a new park, the size of 68 football fields in the sea off England. It is the second longest train tunnel in the world, after the Seikan Tunnel in Japan, just 4 kilometers longer.

Thanks to the Channel Tunnel, it takes just 20 minutes to travel between England and France. Due to the shorter traveling time, both England and France have benefited by using the tunnel.

영국과 프랑스 사이에 터널을 만들고자 시도한 최초의 사람은 나폴레옹이었다. 그러나 굉장히 시간이 오래 걸렸다. 그리고 나서 1994년에 두 나라를 하나로 연결하는 Channel Tunnel이라 불리는 50km 길이의 터널이 마침내 완공되었다.

15,000명이 넘는 사람들이 7년에 걸쳐 터널을 완공했다. 파헤쳐진 흙은 영국의 바다에 새로 68개의 축구장만한 크기의 공원을 짓는데 사용되었다. 그것은 4km 더 긴 일본의 Seikan 터널 다음으로 세계에서 두 번째로 긴 기차터널이다.

Channel Tunnel 덕분에 영국과 프랑스 사이를 여행하는 데는 20분밖에 걸리지 않는다. 좀더 줄어든 여행시간 때문에 영국과 프랑스 모두 터널을 사용함으로써 큰 이익을 보고 있다.

Basic Drills 1

Listen and choose the correct answer. MP3 50-51

1 What is compared between the tower and other buildings?

(A) Their angles
(B) Their popularity
(C) Pictures taken from them

🎧 Listen again and fill in the blanks.

> Buildings and towers _____ _____ _____.
> However, there is one very famous tower _____ _____. The Leaning Tower of Pisa in Italy currently leans _____ _____ _____. The tower started leaning because it was built _____ _____ _____. Even though the tower is leaning, many people _____ _____ of the tower.

2 What is compared between the pyramids and a football field?

(A) Their function
(B) Their size
(C) Their design

🎧 Listen again and fill in the blanks.

> _____ _____ _____ _____ of the world are the pyramids in Egypt. The pyramids are _____ for Egyptian kings and queens. The pyramids are very big, even bigger than _____ _____ _____. The entrances to the pyramids are very complicated, as the designers did not want people _____ _____ the Pharaoh's gold.

Basic Drills 2

Taking Notes: Key Words (I) - 핵심어

노트필기는 청취 지문의 이해와 기억을 돕기 위한 것이므로 글의 내용을 그대로 다 받아 적을 필요가 없다. 효율적인 노트필기를 위해 요지를 잘 드러내는 핵심 단어만을 적는다. 핵심어는 관사, 전치사, 접속사와 같은 기능어보다는 주로 동사, 명사, 형용사 등의 내용어를 구분하여 노트한다.

> Whales are not actually fish, but are the largest mammals in the world.
> Key words: whales not fish, largest mammals

On Your Own

1. Read the sentences below and underline the key words.

    (1) Earth is the third planet from the sun.

    (2) He knew how to fly the plane.

    (3) Cars and buses cause pollution to the environment.

2. Listen and take notes using key words, symbols and abbreviations. [MP3 52]

    (1) _____
    (2) _____
    (3) _____

Listening Practice 1

Listen and choose the correct answer. As you listen, try to catch the hidden information.

Weather can be ~~~~~~~~~~ to the other, if they are ~~~~~~~~ ~~~~~~. Some countries ~~~~~~~~, while other countries ~~~~~~. This is one reason ~~~~~~~~~~~~~~~~~~~~, such as Alaska. Many people visit Alaska ~~~~~~~~~~~~.

Alaska has ~~~~~~~~~~~~ between summer and winter. ~~~~~~ ~~~~~~~ recorded was over 37°C. ~~~~~~~~~~ recorded was -62°C. It can get really cold in Alaska.

Alaska also has ~~~~~~~~~~~~~~ from the rest of the world. Sometimes, the sun ~~~~~~~~~~. This is why ~~~~~~~~~~~~ to visitors. In some parts of Alaska, ~~~~~~~~~~~~~~~~.

1 What is the passage mainly about?

(A) The different time in Alaska
(B) The location of Alaska
(C) The coldest temperature in Alaska
(D) The characteristics of Alaska

2 What comparison is made between Alaska and other places?

(A) The temperature during winter
(B) The times of sunset
(C) The short nights during summer
(D) The number of visitors during the night

Listening Practice 2

MP3 54

Listen and choose the correct answer. As you listen, try to catch the hidden information.

M: Buildings in US cities are very tall. ~~~~~~~~~~~~~~~~~~~~~~?

W: Not really. Many of the tallest buildings are ~~~~. The Petronas Twin Towers were ~~~~~~~~~~~~~~ in the world. They are ~~~~~~~~~~.

M: ~~~~~~ are the towers?

W: ~~~~~~~~~~ from the ground to the top of the buildings. One of the towers was built ~~~~~~~~~~.

M: That's interesting. ~~~~~~~~~~~~~~~~ in the world?

W: No, ~~~~~~~~~~~~~~~~. The building is called Taipei 101, ~~~~~ ~~~~~~.

M: ~~~~~~~~~~ compared to the Twin Towers?

W: It is ~~~~~~~~. ~~~~~~~~~~~~ is 509 meters. It is shaped ~~~~ ~~~~, and the building is ~~~~~~~~~~~~~~ in Taiwan.

1 What is the conversation mainly about?

(A) The tallest buildings in the world
(B) Taipei 101
(C) The Petronas Twin Towers
(D) The buildings in the US

2 What comparison is made between Taipei 101 and the Petronas Twin Towers?

(A) The age of the buildings
(B) The height of the buildings
(C) The shape of the buildings
(D) The owner of the buildings

Chapter 5. Travel

Listening Practice 3

Listen and choose the correct answer.

MP3 55

Note-taking

---

1 According to the conversation, what will the man see on the tour? Tick in the correct box.

	Yes	No
(A) Famous films with his family		
(B) Actual studios where films are made		
(C) Stars and their families		
(D) The Hollywood Walk of Fame		

2 How does the man describe the tour of Hollywood?

(A) By listing the streets and then studios
(B) By identifying studios and then what to see
(C) By mentioning the places to visit and then what to see
(D) By mentioning the streets and then his plans

Listening Practice 4

Listen and choose the correct answer.

MP3 56

Note-taking

1 What is the talk mainly about?

(A) Where to wash in India
(B) Where to sleep in India
(C) How to get to India
(D) Where to visit in India

2 What is compared between the Ganges and other rivers around the world?

(A) The length of the river
(B) The function of the river
(C) The location of the river
(D) The history of the river

Listening Practice 5

Listen and choose the correct answer.

MP3 57

Note-taking

1 According to the talk, what is Big Ben?

(A) It is the name of a very large bell.
(B) It is the name of a tall clock tower.
(C) It is the name of an English palace.
(D) It is the name of a palace gate.

2 What is compared between Buckingham Palace and Istana Nurul Iman?

(A) The people in the palaces
(B) The gates of the palaces
(C) The size of the palaces
(D) The guards in the palaces

Listening Practice 6

Listen and choose the correct answer.

MP3 58

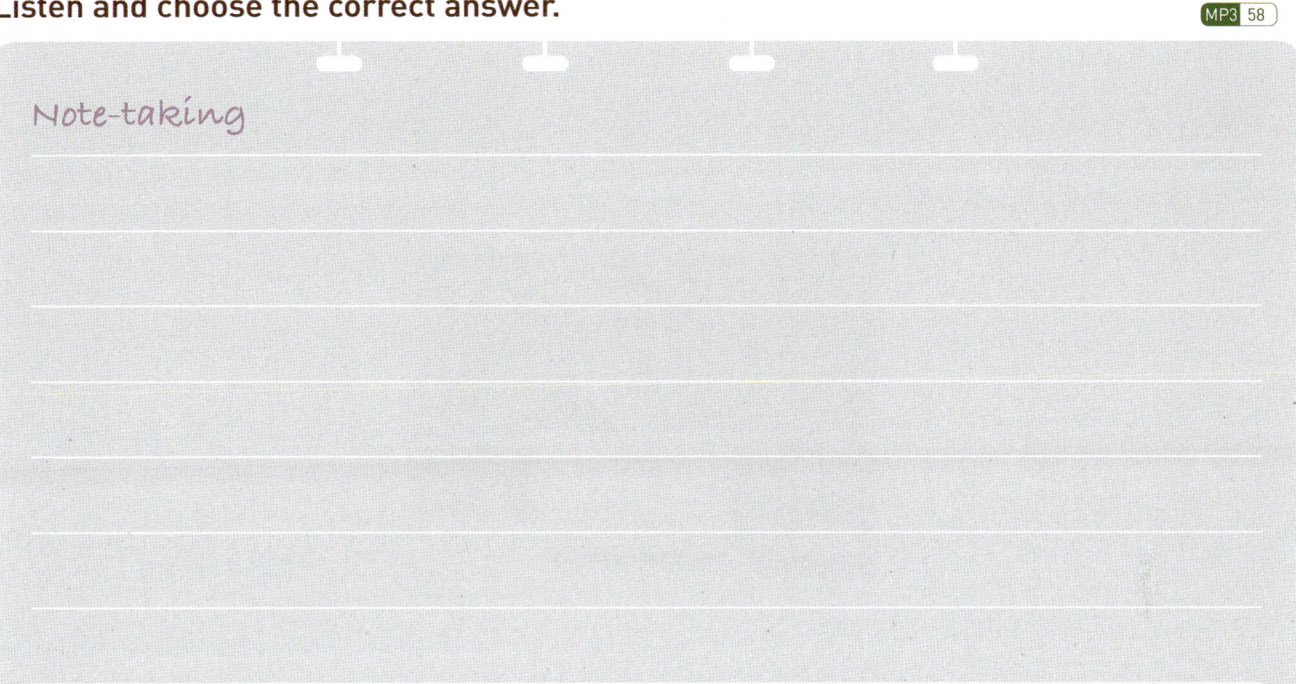

Note-taking

1 What is compared between the Amazon and the Nile?

(A) The type of animals in the rivers
(B) The width of the rivers
(C) The amount of animals in the rivers
(D) The length of the rivers

2 How does the speaker talk about anacondas?

(A) By identifying how the anaconda lives in the river
(B) By contrasting with other snakes
(C) By listing the characteristics of an anaconda
(D) By giving examples of what anacondas eat

iBT Practice 1

TOEFL Listening

1. What is the talk mainly about?

   A Big rocks and the stars
   B The mysteries of Stonehenge
   C Things in England
   D Watching the stars

2. According to the teacher, what did people think of Stonehenge after they found human bones?

   A They thought Stonehenge might be for scientists to work.
   B They thought Stonehenge might be a place to watch stars.
   C They thought Stonehenge might be just a circle.
   D They thought Stonehenge might be a cemetery.

TOEFL Listening

Note-taking

3 What is compared between the stones and buses?

Ⓐ Their height
Ⓑ Their weight
Ⓒ Their size
Ⓓ Their length

iBT Practice 2

TOEFL Listening

1 According to the woman, what will she do in Thailand?
Tick in the correct box.

	Yes	No
Ⓐ Snorkeling in the sea		
Ⓑ Eating bananas on the boat		
Ⓒ Eating a lot of seafood		
Ⓓ Scuba diving under the sea		

2 Why does the man mention jet skis?

　　Ⓐ To tell the woman to buy a jet ski
　　Ⓑ To emphasize that there are many things to try
　　Ⓒ To warn the woman that it is dangerous
　　Ⓓ To find out if she is going to ride a jet ski

TOEFL Listening

Note-taking

3 What comparison does the woman make between scuba diving and snorkeling?

- Ⓐ What corals she can see
- Ⓑ How many fish she can see
- Ⓒ How dangerous it is
- Ⓓ Who can scuba dive and snorkel

Dictation

iBT Practice 1

Listen and fill in the blanks. MP3 59

_____ _____ are very heavy, so we need a lot of people to _____ _____. This is why _____ _____ _____ is such an amazing creation.

The stones in Stonehenge are _____ _____ _____ buses. We do not know _____ _____ _____ the heavy stones to Stonehenge. We do not even know what Stonehenge _____ _____ _____. Some scientists believe that Stonehenge was used for _____ _____ _____ in the sky. This is because the stones seem to follow _____ _____ of the stars at night.

Others believe that Stonehenge was used _____ _____ _____. We don't know if _____ _____ _____ in Stonehenge, but _____ _____ were found in the circle. This made people think that Stonehenge might have been _____ _____ at the same time. Perhaps we will never know _____ _____ _____ Stonehenge was built, but it does not matter. Many people still _____ _____ _____ the amazing stones.

iBT Practice 2

Listen and fill in the blanks. MP3 60

M: Where are you going for _____ _____ _____?

W: My family is _____ _____ _____ to the beach in Thailand.

M: That _____ _____. What are you _____ _____ _____ on the beach?

W: Well, I was trying _____ _____ whether I should go _____ _____ or snorkeling. _____ _____ _____ scuba diving is dangerous, so I am going to snorkel. It's _____ _____ scuba diving, and I still get to see _____ _____.

M: I guess there will be a lot of _____ _____ on the beach as well. People are always trying _____ _____ _____ there. There are always _____ _____ for people to ride, too.

W: Yes, but I would like to sit on _____ _____ _____. It looks like a lot of fun.

M: That sounds great. _____ _____ will you be doing?

W: Oh, I guess I _____ _____ _____ a lot! Thailand has many types _____ _____. I can't wait _____ _____ _____. I'm so excited!

M: Do me a favor and _____ _____ _____ when you're there. I'd really love to see _____ _____ _____ in Thailand.

Match the words from the box with the definitions.

| dig | lean | pagoda | function |
| poison | drown | squeeze | cemetery |

1 _____ to move into a sloping position; not to be upright

2 _____ to press something together, usually with your fingers or hand

3 _____ to kill someone by pushing them under water

4 _____ the purpose that something has, or the job that someone or something does

5 _____ a place where dead people are buried

6 _____ a substance that can kill you or make you sick when taken into the body

7 _____ a building used for religious purposes, especially by Buddhists, and usually highly decorated

8 _____ to make a hole in the ground using your hands or a tool

Choose the best phrase to fit in each one of the blanks.

| at an angle | compared to | look forward to | in front of |

9 There is plenty of room to park on the street _____ our house.

10 We _____ seeing our relatives when they arrive for a family reunion.

11 Keep your hands at the back of your head and slowly raise your leg _____ of 45 degree.

12 The Wright brothers' original aircraft was tiny _____ a modern jet airliner.

106 b-Listening

useful Phrasal Verbs

+ **hand out** 나누어주다
People **handed out** information about the museum when we entered.

+ **hand over** 넘겨주다
Jill **handed over** the pencil to Peter after she used it.

+ **hold on** 기다리다
Hold on a second. I'll get it for you.

+ **keep on** 계속하다
I think I should **keep on** working until he comes back.

+ **keep up** 유지하다
It is hard to **keep up** the pace in a marathon race.

+ **lay down** 눕히다
She carefully **laid down** her baby in the cradle.

+ **lay off** 해고하다
The factory will **lay off** 10 staff members as the number of tourists has decreased.

+ **leave out** 제외시키다
Teachers are always careful not to **leave out** anyone in their class.

+ **look after** 보살피다
The babysitter has been **looking after** the children for many years.

+ **look for** ~을 찾다
Brad was out at night to **look for** his dog which ran away.

+ **look forward to** ~을 기대하다
We are **looking forward to** the camp.

Chapter 6
Food

Topic:
Food

Question Type:
Content-Linking Questions
내용 연결 확인 문제
언급된 사항들간의 관계를 파악하는 문제

Content-Linking Questions
내용 연결 확인 문제

1. 내용 연결 확인 문제에서는 들려 주는 글의 내용에서 분명하게 암시되어 있거나 언급된 하나 이상의 서로 다른 정보를 연결하여 종합하는 능력을 평가한다. 원인과 결과에 대한 내용들을 추론하거나 결과를 예측, 또는 일반화시키는 등의 내용 추론을 묻는다.

2. 추론이란 직접 언급되지 않은 내용을 생각하여 파악하는 것을 말한다.

3. 반드시 지문에서 명시적으로 언급된 내용을 근거로만 추측해야 한다. 주어진 정보가 아닌 자신이 개인적으로 알고 있는 정보를 이용해 문제를 풀어서는 안 된다.

- What does the man imply about sheep's head?
- What can be inferred about lobsters?

Sample Question MP3 61

TOEFL Listening VOLUME HELP OK NEXT HIDE TIME 00:10:00

What does the teacher imply about non-Hindu vegetarians?

Ⓐ They think eating meat is healthier.
Ⓑ They think eating meat is cruel.
Ⓒ They like to give orders to other people.
Ⓓ They want to become Hindus.

Sctipt & 해석

　Meat is the main dish of many cultures and countries. Most people cannot imagine living without meat. Yet there are people who live without eating meat at all. These people are called vegetarians.

　A lot of vegetarians only eat vegetables because of their religion. Hinduism is one of the religions of the world that teaches followers not to eat meat. Although some Hindus eat meat, they still do not eat beef as cows are considered holy in Hinduism.

　There are also some vegetarians who are not Hindus. They do not eat meat for personal reasons. These vegetarians often try to get other people to stop eating meat so that fewer animals will suffer.

　고기는 많은 문화권과 많은 나라에서 주식이다. 대부분의 사람들은 고기 없이 살아가는 것을 상상할 수 없다. 그러나 고기를 전혀 먹지 않고 사는 사람도 있다. 이 사람들을 일컬어 채식주의자라고 한다.

　상당수의 채식주의자는 종교 때문에 채소만 먹는다. 힌두교는 신도들에게 육식을 금하도록 가르치는 세계 종교 중 하나이다. 어떤 힌두교도는 고기를 먹지만, 힌두교에서는 소를 신성하게 여기기 때문에 쇠고기는 먹지 않는다.

　힌두교가 아닌데도 채식주의자인 사람들이 있다. 그들은 개인적인 이유로 고기를 먹지 않는다. 이런 채식주의자들은 동물들이 고통을 덜 받게 하기 위해 사람들이 고기 먹는 것을 그만두게 하기 위해 노력을 한다.

Basic Drills 1

Listen and choose the correct answer. MP3 62-63

1 What does the man imply about seafood?

(A) He does not eat seafood often.
(B) He likes seafood a lot.
(C) He prefers seafood to meat.

🎧 Listen again and fill in the blanks.

> W: What is your _____ _____? I love eating seafood.
> M: I prefer steak and other types of meat.
> W: Doctors say that red meat, _____ _____ _____, has a lot of cholesterol and fat. We should not eat _____ _____ of that.
> M: Well, I guess you're right. Still, _____ _____ _____ _____. I love the taste of steak.

2 What is implied about Italians making noodles into spaghetti?

(A) The Italians did not want to copy the Chinese style of noodles.
(B) The Italians did not want to change the taste of the noodles.
(C) The Italians had to change the ingredients of their noodles.

🎧 Listen again and fill in the blanks.

> One of the most popular dishes _____ _____ is spaghetti. But many say that spaghetti is originally from China. Chinese chefs made noodles many years _____ _____ _____, and Italian merchants like Marco Polo brought them back to Italy. Since the vegetables and meat in China were _____ _____ those in Italy, the Italians made _____ _____ into spaghetti.

Basic Drills 2

Taking Notes: Key Words (II) - 핵심어

청취 지문을 듣고 난 후 문제를 풀 때 중요 내용을 명확하게 기억할 수 있도록 돕기 위해서 노트필기를 한다. 이때 간단한 구나 어휘를 사용하여 핵심 내용만을 적는다.

Example:

We are going to the park on Sunday for a picnic.

Key words: we R → park Sun. picnc

On Your Own

1. Read the sentences. Use symbols, abbreviations, and key words to write the sentences as short as possible.

   (1) Polar bears are able to live in extremely cold areas because of their fur.
      → _____

   (2) The invention of the pocket watch brought great changes in sea travel.
      → _____

   (3) Lack of oxygen and quick forming storms are the greatest dangers to climbers.
      → _____

2. Listen and write down the sentence as short as possible. **MP3 64**

   (1) _____
   (2) _____
   (3) _____

Listening Practice 1

Listen and choose the correct answer. As you listen, try to catch the hidden information.

~~~~~~~~~~~~~~~~~~~~~~ are everywhere in large cities. This is ~~~~~~~~~, and it can ~~~~~~~~~~~~~~. However, ~~~~~~~~~~~~~~~~~~ about them. ~~~~~~~~~~~~~~~~~~ used in fast food restaurants are ~~~~~~~~~~~. Foods from these restaurants are ~~~~~~~~~~~~~~~~~~~~. It would not be so bad if we ~~~~~~~~~~~~~. But a lot of the people ~~~~~~~~~~~~~~~~~~~ and do not exercise.

Fast foods also ~~~~~~~~~~~~~~~~~~~. There are ~~~~~~~~~~~ in the menu. If we ~~~~~~~~~~~~~~~, then we should make sure that ~~~~~~~~~~~~~~~~. Fortunately, many of the fast food companies are ~~~~~~~~~~~~~~~~~~. The next time you go into a fast food restaurant, ~~~~~~~~~~~~~~~~~~~~~~~~.

1 What is the passage mainly about?

(A) The good points of fast food restaurants
(B) The bad points of fast food restaurants
(C) The salads in fast food restaurants
(D) The convenience of fast food restaurants

2 What is implied about fast food restaurants?

(A) We should eat fast food often.
(B) We should not order the salad.
(C) We should think about a balanced diet.
(D) We should be overweight to eat fast food.

Listening Practice 2

MP3 66

Listen and choose the correct answer. As you listen, try to catch the hidden information.

A lot of people around the world ~~~~~~~~~~~~~~~~~~~~~~~~~. In many parts of Asia, they eat ~~~~~~~~~~~~~~. A popular food ~~~~~~~~~~~~~~~. There are ~~~~~~~~~~. Ginseng usually ~~~~~~~~~~ and is used ~~~~~~~~~~~~. Ginseng can be grown ~~~~~~~~~~~~, including the US, China, and even France. Wild oriental ginseng, ~~~~~~~~~~~~, is expensive and ~~~~~~~ even in shops. Some people spend a lot of time ~~~~~~~. This type of ginseng takes ~~~~~~~~~~~. Some wild ginseng can be ~~~~~~~~~.

1 What is the talk mainly about?

(A) Different types of ginseng
(B) The benefits of ginseng
(C) The colors of ginseng
(D) The strength of ginseng

2 What is implied about ginseng?

(A) Many people think it is for old people.
(B) Many people think it only grows in Asia.
(C) Many people think it is effective.
(D) Many people think it is common.

Listening Practice 3

Listen and choose the correct answer.

MP3 67

Note-taking

---

1 What is implied about salmon in Japan?

(A) There are many salmon caught in Japan.
(B) They are always cooked before eating.
(C) Many salmon are exported to Norway.
(D) There are no salmon caught in Japan.

2 According to the conversation, which of the following are true about the Japanese? Tick in the correct box.

	Yes	No
(A) Japanese prefer chicken to fish.		
(B) Most Japanese food is based on fish.		
(C) Most Japanese like tuna.		
(D) Japanese go to Sweden to eat salmon.		

Listening Practice 4

Listen and choose the correct answer.

MP3 68

Note-taking

1. What will the speaker probably do if he is offered puffer fish?

   (A) He will not eat the fish.
   (B) He will eat the fish.
   (C) He will eat the liver and skin.
   (D) He will train more chefs.

2. Why does the speaker mention that only trained chefs can prepare the puffer fish?

   (A) To contrast how people eat the fish
   (B) To give examples of where the fish are caught
   (C) To emphasize that the fish is dangerous
   (D) To mention that the fish looks funny

Chapter 6. Food

Listening Practice 5

Listen and choose the correct answer.

Note-taking

1 What is the conversation mainly about?

(A) Foods of different cultures
(B) Messages of different cultures
(C) Differences of cakes
(D) Ways of cooking special foods

2 Listen again to part of the conversation. Then answer the question.
What is inferred about American Indians?

(A) The Indians used to raise turkeys.
(B) The Pilgrims had turkey with the Indians.
(C) The Indians helped the Pilgrims hunt turkeys.
(D) Turkey was a traditional food of the Indians.

Listening Practice 6

Listen and choose the correct answer.

Note-taking

1 What is the talk mainly about?

(A) Different people that enjoy ice cream
(B) Different ingredients of ice cream
(C) Different desserts of the world
(D) Different histories of ice cream

2 What can be inferred about ice cream?

(A) The origin of ice cream is well-known.
(B) No one knows the origin of ice cream.
(C) Ice cream was made by a royal family.
(D) Nobody enjoyed eating ice cream.

*i*BT Practice 1

TOEFL Listening

1. How does the speaker talk about foods?

   Ⓐ By contrasting with other foods
   Ⓑ By listing fried foods in the US
   Ⓒ By giving examples of unusual foods
   Ⓓ By mentioning them in time order

2. According to the speaker, what do some Americans eat in the US?

   Ⓐ They eat fried bats.
   Ⓑ They eat fried duck.
   Ⓒ They eat foie gras.
   Ⓓ They eat rattlesnake meat.

TOEFL Listening

Note-taking

3 What is implied about foie gras?

Ⓐ It is cruel to ducks.
Ⓑ It is not very tasty.
Ⓒ It is eaten by rattlesnakes.
Ⓓ It comes from bats.

iBT Practice 2

TOEFL Listening

1. What is the conversation mainly about?

   Ⓐ Different cows of the world
   Ⓑ Different animals in Nepal
   Ⓒ Different taste of goat meat
   Ⓓ Different milk of animals

2. According to the conversation, which of the following are true about goat's milk? Tick in the correct box.

	Yes	No
Ⓐ Goat's milk is sweeter than cow's milk.		
Ⓑ Goat's milk is popular in Nepal.		
Ⓒ Everyone likes goat's milk.		
Ⓓ Indians think goat's milk can cure sickness.		

TOEFL Listening

Note-taking

3. Listen again to part of the conversation. Then answer the question. What is inferred about yak's milk?

Ⓐ Not everyone likes the taste.
Ⓑ Everyone likes the taste.
Ⓒ It is better than goat's milk.
Ⓓ Yak milk is always cold.

Dictation

iBT Practice 1

Listen and fill in the blanks. MP3 71

Some countries enjoy _____ _____ that other countries _____ _____ _____ at all. Here are some countries with very different ideas of _____ _____ _____.

In Texas, U.S.A., _____ _____ _____ for rattlesnake meat. The meat is coated _____ _____ and _____ in very hot oil. It is a very _____ _____ in Texas, and some of the people say that rattlesnake meat is _____ _____ _____ in the world.

Small shops in the streets of Thailand _____ _____ _____. The bat is _____ _____, so that people can still see _____ _____ _____ and head on it. It is not _____ _____, because it is hard _____ _____ the bats.

The people in France eat _____ _____ _____ as foie gras, meaning _____ _____. The liver mostly _____ _____ _____, although it was _____ _____ _____. The farmers _____ _____ _____ to eat a lot of corn for 4 to 5 months. This makes the liver _____ _____. Many people want this _____ _____, because they say that the ducks _____ _____ _____.

iBT Practice 2

Listen and fill in the blanks. MP3 72

M: Look at _____ _____ _____ from the store today. It's _____ _____.

W: Yak? What's that?

M: It's _____ _____ _____ cow. Well, they aren't really cows _____ _____ _____ in milk farms. Yaks are big animals that live mostly _____ _____ _____ in Asia, such as Nepal and _____ _____ _____. They are used for _____ _____ _____ across mountains.

W: Wow, I didn't know that. Why _____ _____ _____ yak's milk?

M: A lot of people think eating food from a strong animal _____ _____ _____. The one bad point is that the taste might be _____ _____ for some people.

W: Well, I have tried _____ _____, and I'm crazy about it. It was _____ _____. I think goat's milk is _____ _____ cow's milk. I think _____ _____ _____ a bottle of goat's milk tomorrow.

M: Oh yeah. Goat's milk is very popular, too. A lot of _____ _____ _____ drink goat's milk. Indians think that goat's milk can _____ _____ _____, so many sick people drink goat's milk _____ _____. But again, not everyone likes goat's milk.

Chapter 6. Food

Word Review

Match the words from the box with the definitions.

| vegetarian | convenience | regularly | overweight |
| raw | import | recipe | region |

1 _____ heavier than you should be

2 _____ someone who does not eat meat or fish

3 _____ to buy a product from another country and bring it to your country

4 _____ not cooked; being in a natural state or not prepared for use

5 _____ a part of a country, the world, etc.

6 _____ at the same time each day, week, month, etc.

7 _____ a condition that is useful by making something easier or saving you time

8 _____ a set of statements or an explanation that tells how to cook a particular food

Choose the best phrase to fit in each one of the blanks.

| including | is based on | depend on | up to |

9 Most of the people in the area _____ fishing for their living.

10 I will have four exams in this course _____ the midterm and final.

11 The weather forecast says we are expecting _____ 30 cm of snow this coming weekend.

12 The movie _____ the book, but the book gives more detailed information.

useful Phrasal Verbs

- **look over** 검사하다, 진찰하다
  The doctor **looked over** the patient before the operation.

- **look up** ~을 찾아보다
  I don't know what that word means. I'll have to **look** it **up** in the dictionary.

- **make out** 알아보다
  The teacher could not **make out** who was behind the door.

- **make up** ~를 만들다
  The student **made up** a story about the dog eating his homework.

- **mix up** ~ 때문에 혼동되다, 헷갈리다
  I couldn't finish the report because the directions **mixed** me **up**.

- **nod off** 졸다
  The audience **nodded off** during the speech.

- **pass away** 죽다
  Everyone was grieving when the Pope **passed away**.

- **pick out** 고르다
  We had a hard time **picking out** what to wear to the prom.

- **pick up** 집어들다
  She **picked up** the apple from the table.

- **put away** 저장하다, 모으다
  She **put away** the cereal and milk bottles.

- **put off** 미루다
  He **put off** his homework for another day.

Chapter 6. Food

Chapter 7
Art & Entertainment

Topic:
Art & Entertainment

Question Type:
Stance/Attitude Questions
입장/태도 파악 문제
화자의 태도를 파악하는 문제

Stance/Attitude Questions

입장/태도 파악 문제

1. 지문의 일부분을 다시 들려 주고 그 중 한 문장 또는 특정 표현에서 알 수 있는 화자의 입장(stance)이나 태도(attitude)를 묻는 문제이다. 주어진 사실에 대해 화자가 어떠한 태도를 갖고 말하고 있는가 또는 화자가 그 사실에 대해 말할 때 어느 정도의 확신을 갖고 말하는가에 대한 이해 능력을 평가 한다.

2. 🎧 표시가 나오면서 들려준 지문의 내용 중에서 일부분을 한번 더 들려주고 그 부분에 대한 질문을 하기도 한다.

> - What is the woman's attitude toward Picasso's paintings?
> - What does the man mean when he says this: 🎧

Sample Question

TOEFL Listening

What is the teacher's attitude toward computer art?

Ⓐ He does not like drawing with computers.
Ⓑ He thinks it is hard to use computers to draw.
Ⓒ He is sure that old-fashioned art is better.
Ⓓ He thinks it is easier to draw with computers.

Sctipt & 해석

People always think that art is painting on canvas or paper. Traditional artists only used their hands and brush to paint. Recently, thanks to technology, there are new artists that use computers to draw instead.

Computer graphics experts use either the mouse or the keyboard instead of the brush to create and draw pictures. It is much easier to choose the correct colors and draw shapes of objects. Computer programs are so easy to use that there are new artists that create pictures with their computers.

If old-fashioned painters made a mistake, they would have to either start to do it again, or try to hide the mistake by painting over it. In computer art, all the artist needs to do is simply click a button.

사람들은 언제나 캔버스나 종이 위에 그린 그림이 예술이라고 생각한다. 예전의 화가들은 그림을 그리기 위해 손과 붓을 사용하였다. 최근에는 기술의 발전 덕에 그림을 그리는데 컴퓨터를 사용하는 새로운 예술가들이 생겨나고 있다.

컴퓨터 그래픽 전문가는 창작을 하거나 그림을 그리기 위해 붓 대신에 마우스나 키보드를 사용한다. 적합한 색을 고르고 형태를 그려가는 것이 훨씬 더 수월해졌다. 컴퓨터 프로그램이 사용하기 매우 편리해서 컴퓨터로 작업하는 새로운 예술가들이 생겨나고 있다.

예전의 화가들은 뭔가 실수를 하면 다시 처음부터 시작하거나 그 위에 덧칠을 함으로써 실수한 부분을 숨겼다. 컴퓨터 예술에서 화가가 해야 하는 것은 마우스 버튼을 클릭하는 것이 전부이다.

Basic Drills 1

Listen and choose the correct answer. MP3 74-75

1 What is the speaker's attitude toward the finding of cave paintings?

(A) She is confused.
(B) She is angry.
(C) She is pleased.

🎧 Listen again and fill in the blanks.

> The oldest pictures in the world are paintings _____ _____
> _____. They were drawn _____ _____ _____
> ago by people that lived in the caves. They drew pictures of animals and _____
> _____ _____ for them. It was great that we found the drawings,
> as the pictures helped professors understand _____ _____
> _____.

2 What does the woman mean when she says this: 🎧

(A) She did not notice Mona Lisa on television.
(B) She did not know that Mona Lisa did not have eyebrows.
(C) She is sure that she knew about Mona Lisa's eyebrows.

🎧 Listen again and fill in the blanks.

> M: Did you know _____ _____ _____ of Mona Lisa
> does not have eyebrows?
> W: Are you sure? I've seen it many times _____ _____, but I didn't
> notice.
> M: It's true. Moreover, some also say _____ _____
> _____ in the picture might not even be smiling. _____
> _____ some call her the lady with the mysterious smile.

Basic Drills 2

Taking Notes: **Signal Words (I) - 표시어**

표시어란 들려주는 글의 내용과 정보간의 관계를 나타내는 말이다. 표시어를 잘 들으면 효율적으로 효과적인 노트필기를 할 수 있다.

1. Signal words for examples
   : for example, for instance, as an example, etc.
2. Signal words for supporting ideas
   : First ..., second ..., third ..., a major point, most importantly, etc.

On Your Own

1. Read the passage and underline the signal words or phrases.

   > We must remember the three rules of soccer. First, we must not touch the ball with our hands. Second, the ball must not go out of the white line. Third, we must start in the middle of the field after we score a goal.

2. Listen carefully for the signal words. Write down all the signal words that you hear. **MP3 76**

   _____

   _____

3. Listen again and write your notes by using the signal words, symbols, abbreviations, and key words if necessary. **MP3 77**

Chapter 7. Art & Entertainment 133

Listening Practice

Listen and choose the correct answer. As you listen, try to catch the hidden information.

When people talk ~~~~~~, they think about paintings ~~~~. However, ~~~~~~~. As long as ~~~~~~~, it can be called art.

There are some artists ~~~~~~. People pay ~~~~~~ by special painters. A lot of the paintings on cars are ~~~~~~. Most of the work looks ~~~~~~.

Tattoo artists "draw" ~~~~~~~~. The machine has ~~~~~~. There are ~~~~~~, as more people around the world ~~~~~. Tattoos done by famous artists can look ~~~~~~.

1 What is implied about more people wanting tattoos?

(A) Many people do not want tattoos.
(B) Many people are getting tattoos.
(C) Many people want fire tattoos.
(D) Many people want tattoos of their cars.

2 What is the speaker's attitude toward art not drawn on paper?

(A) She does not think it is real art.
(B) She does not know about it.
(C) She thinks it is too difficult.
(D) She thinks that it is great art.

Listening Practice 2

Listen and choose the correct answer. As you listen, try to catch the hidden information.

> There are many ways that ~~~~~~~~~~ to others, sometimes ~~~~~~~~~~.
>
> There are ~~~~~~~~~~ in the US and Europe. These people ~~~~~~~~~~ and make people laugh. The differences between clowns and mimes are that ~~~~~~~~~~, and they neither ~~~~~~~~~~. They only ~~~~~~~~~~ what they are trying to express.
>
> Another good performance is ~~~~~~~~~~. One-man bands have ~~~~~~~~~~. When they move their bodies, it will either ~~~~~~~~~~. They are ~~~~~~~~~~ to watch. ~~~~~~~~~~, one-man band performers ~~~~~~~~~~.

1 What does the teacher imply about one-man bands disappearing?

(A) She is happy about them disappearing.
(B) She prefers clowns to one-man bands.
(C) She is sad about them disappearing.
(D) She does not express any emotions.

2 How does the teacher talk about performers?

(A) By listing different clowns
(B) By mentioning the performers in other countries
(C) By describing their performances
(D) By mentioning their popularity

Listening Practice 3

Listen and choose the correct answer.

MP3 80

Note-taking

1 What is the woman's attitude toward Picasso's paintings?

(A) She does not like Picasso's paintings.
(B) She likes Picasso's paintings as much as Monet's.
(C) She likes Picasso's paintings better than Monet's.
(D) She wants to buy Picasso's paintings.

2 What is compared between Picasso's and Monet's art?

(A) When their paintings were done
(B) What their paintings are called
(C) How easy it is to understand
(D) Who likes their paintings

Listening Practice

Listen and choose the correct answer.

Note-taking

1 What does the teacher imply about photography?

(A) He does not think it is good to take pictures.
(B) He thinks it's a great way to express oneself.
(C) He thinks that there is little information on it.
(D) He does not think photographers are artists.

2 According to the teacher, what do beginners need to start photography?

(A) Beginners need chemicals.
(B) Beginners need paintings.
(C) Beginners need a camera.
(D) Beginners need the internet.

Listening Practice 5

Listen and choose the correct answer.

MP3 82

Note-taking

1 What is the discussion mainly about?

(A) Different types of dances
(B) Different types of paintings
(C) Different types of singers
(D) Different types of art

2 Listen again to part of the discussion. Then answer the question. What does the man mean when he says this: 🎧

(A) He thinks that paintings are not art.
(B) He does not know what paintings are.
(C) He thought only paintings were called art.
(D) He wants to know what art is.

Listening Practice 6

Listen and choose the correct answer.

MP3 83

Note-taking

1 What is the talk mainly about?

(A) Location of clown universities
(B) Students in clown universities
(C) Popularity of clown universities
(D) Lessons in clown universities

2 What does the speaker mean when he says this:

(A) People expect clowns to laugh.
(B) People expect clowns to be funny.
(C) People want clowns to open a university.
(D) People try to make clowns speak.

iBT Practice 1

1 According to the conversation, which of the following are true about the man? Tick in the correct box.

	Yes	No
Ⓐ He read a book about magic.		
Ⓑ He knows that magicians do real magic.		
Ⓒ He thinks that magic is boring.		
Ⓓ He wanted to be a magician.		

2 Why does the woman mention that magicians practice for years?

   Ⓐ To list the names of tricks that magicians perform
   Ⓑ To give examples of how magic tricks are done
   Ⓒ To introduce a famous magician
   Ⓓ To stress that magic tricks can be very hard

TOEFL Listening

Note-taking

3 Listen again to part of the conversation. Then answer the question. What does the man mean when he says this: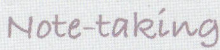

- Ⓐ He does not know any magic tricks.
- Ⓑ He wants to show the girl magic tricks.
- Ⓒ He wrote a book about magic tricks.
- Ⓓ He made some new magic tricks.

*i*BT Practice 2

TOEFL Listening

1. According to the teacher, why are Shakespeare's plays hard to understand?

    Ⓐ Shakespeare did not use English.
    Ⓑ Shakespeare was a bad writer.
    Ⓒ Shakespeare used old English.
    Ⓓ Shakespeare did not write a list of hard words.

2. What does the woman imply about the list of words?

    Ⓐ She thinks that the list did not help her.
    Ⓑ She thinks that the list might help the man.
    Ⓒ She is sure that the list is helpful to everyone.
    Ⓓ She does not know how to make the reading easier.

TOEFL Listening

Note-taking

3 What will the man probably do?

Ⓐ He will get a word list from the woman.
Ⓑ He will write a play of his own.
Ⓒ He will not read Shakespeare's plays anymore.
Ⓓ He will try to read Shakespeare's plays again.

Dictation

iBT Practice 1

Listen and fill in the blanks. MP3 84

M: I heard that _____ _____ _____ is coming to school today.

W: Yes, that is _____. I saw his show about a month ago _____ _____. He is very good with _____ _____.

M: Really? I _____ _____ _____ magic shows. I know they are _____ _____, but I still enjoy watching _____ _____ in the magician's hands. _____ _____ what they can do.

W: I _____ _____ _____. They always have so much fun _____ _____ with their wonderful tricks.

M: Yes, I even thought about _____ _____ _____ when I was younger. I wish I could do some tricks _____ _____ _____. I read a book about magic _____ _____ _____. Some tricks looked _____ _____, but most of them looked _____ _____ to do.

W: That is because it takes _____ _____ _____ to be a very good magician. Not everyone can do magic tricks _____ _____ _____ magicians can. Anyway, I guess I'll see you _____ _____ _____ later. I have to go to class now.

iBT Practice 2

Listen and fill in the blanks. MP3 85

T: We'll be talking about Shakespeare today. Does anyone know _____ _____ _____?

M: He was _____ _____ _____ that wrote many story books.

W: He didn't write story books. He _____ _____.

T: Yes, very good. He was a writer that wrote plays during _____ _____ _____. Many think of him _____ _____ _____.

W: I _____ _____ that he is a genius. His plays are wonderful. His most famous play, _____ _____ _____, is still what people remember when they _____ _____ _____.

M: I read some of his plays, but they were so _____ _____ _____. They didn't look like they were _____ _____. I nearly _____ up _____ halfway. I don't think I will _____ _____ _____ of his plays.

T: That's because _____ _____ _____ long ago, and the English language was a little bit _____ _____ _____. For example, "thy" _____ _____, and "thou" _____ _____. Once you _____ _____ _____ it, it's not too difficult to understand it.

W: It was hard for me, too, but I made _____ _____ _____ words. It _____ _____ _____ for everyone, but it helped me understand the play better. You should give Shakespeare _____ _____.

M: Yes, maybe I should do that.

Chapter 7. Art & Entertainment

Word Review

Match the words from the box with the definitions.

| expert | tattoo | instrument | entertaining |
| chemical | develop | trick | disappear |

1. _____ to become impossible to see

2. _____ enjoyable or fun to do

3. _____ someone who has a special skill or knowledge of a subject

4. _____ a picture or writing that is drawn on your skin using a needle and ink

5. _____ something you do in order to make someone believe something that is not true

6. _____ a tool used in science, medicine, etc.; an object used for producing music, such as a piano or violin

7. _____ to make a photograph out of a film

8. _____ relating to the way substances react with other substances

Choose the best phrase to fit in each one of the blanks.

| thanks to | is filled with | as well | get used to |

9. We didn't have any trouble _____ your clear instructions.

10. This city has a hot and humid summer, so you must _____ it.

11. While we shop for fresh fruit, let's buy some vegetables _____.

12. The package _____ plastic foam to protect the glasses inside.

146 b-Listening

useful **Phrasal Verbs**

- **put on** 입다, 착용하다
  Pearl **put on** her best dress for her date.

- **put up with** 참다, 견디다
  I can't **put up with** my neighbor's noise every Friday night anymore.

- **run into** 우연히 만나다
  She **ran into** her old friend from kindergarten.

- **run out of** ~이 없어지다, 떨어지다
  We quickly **ran out of** time and couldn't complete the quiz.

- **run over** 훑어보다
  The principal **ran over** the list before going on stage.

- **set out** 시작하다
  The teams **set out** to climb the dangerous mountain.

- **set up** 정리하다
  My sister **set up** her room exactly the way she wanted it.

- **show off** 자랑하다
  Dale **showed off** his cell phone to his friends in school.

- **show up** 나타나다
  Ms. Crawford was very angry when you didn't **show up** for the meeting.

- **shut off** 닫다, 끊어버리다
  We have to **shut off** the gas valve before we leave the house.

- **speak up** 크게 말하다
  You should **speak up** when talking in front of the class.

Chapter 8
Social Issues

Topic:
Social Issues

Question Type:
Function-Purpose Questions
표현 목적 파악 문제
화자가 말한 내용의 의도를 파악하는 문제

Function-Purpose Questions
표현 목적 파악 문제

1. 표현 목적 파악 문제란 화자가 말한 특정 표현의 궁극적인 의도나 의미를 글의 맥락 속에서 이해하는 능력을 묻는 문제이다. 예를 들어, 들려주는 글속에서 "What?"이라는 표현이 놀라움을 나타내기 위함인지, 상대방의 말을 알아듣지 못해서 다시 묻기 위한 의도로 한 말인지에 대해 물어볼 수 있다.

2. Stance/Attitude 문제에서와 같이 🎧 표시가 나오면서 특정 표현을 재생(replay)하여 들려주고 그 부분의 의미 및 말한 의도에 대해 질문할 수 있다.

3. 직설적이고 사실적인 의미 자체 보다는 표현 이면에 숨어 있는 의미에 초점을 맞추어 이해하도록 한다.

- Why does the man says this: 🎧
- Why does the speaker say that many students do not like boarding schools at first?

Sample Question MP3 86

TOEFL Listening

Listen again to part of the conversation.
Then answer the question.
Why does the woman say this: 🎧

- Ⓐ To express that she does not believe the man
- Ⓑ To indicate that the foundation does not do anything
- Ⓒ To show that she has not heard of the foundation
- Ⓓ To say that she believes in the foundation

Sctipt & 해석

W: There are many organizations in this world, and I don't know which one to help.

M: 🎧 Hmm ... have you heard of the Make-A-Wish Foundation? I have given money to them a few times. In my opinion, they work for a very good cause.

W: **I believe I have not. What do they do?**

M: They listen to sick children's wishes and make them come true. In other words, they do this to give hope and happiness to the children.

W: Wow, it sounds like the kids will have more than enough fun. What kinds of wishes do children usually make?

M: Oh, they accept all types of wishes. Wishes can be about meeting a famous star or perhaps going to a special place, such as Disneyland. The foundation tries its best to make sure that the sick children get their wishes to come true.

W: 세상엔 단체들이 참 많아서 어디를 도와야 할 지 모르겠어.

M: 음… 소원을 이루어주는 재단이라고 들어봤어? 그 쪽에 몇 번 돈을 낸 적이 있어. 아주 좋은 목적으로 일하는 단체라고 생각해.

W: 들어본 적이 없는데. 어떤 일을 하는데?

M: 아픈 아이들의 소원을 듣고 그 소원이 이루어지게 해줘. 다시 말해서 아픈 아이들에게 희망과 행복을 주기 위해 이 일을 하는 거지.

W: 우와, 아이들이 즐거워하는 거 이상의 뭔가가 있을 것처럼 들리는데. 아이들이 그 재단에 보통 어떤 종류의 소원을 빌어?

M: 음, 모든 종류의 소원을 들어주지. 소원은 유명한 스타를 만나는 것일 수도 있고 디즈니랜드 같은 특별한 장소에 가는 것일 수도 있어. 그 재단은 아픈 아이들이 자신의 소원을 이루도록 하는데 최선을 다하지.

Basic Drills 1

Listen and choose the correct answer. MP3 87-88

1   Why does the man say this: 🎧

(A) To ask the woman to repeat what she said
(B) To show that he cannot believe the news
(C) To express his happiness about the news

🎧 Listen again and fill in the blanks.

> W: Did you hear that more subjects _____ _____ _____ in school?
>
> M: What? That's impossible. We already have many subjects to study, and there's not _____ _____ for them all.
>
> W: Yes, _____ _____ _____ _____. I think we learn too many subjects already. I wish _____ _____ that students have a really hard time in school with studies.

2   Why does the speaker say this: 🎧

(A) To say that people are angry
(B) To give examples of noise
(C) To list the types of drivers

🎧 Listen again and fill in the blanks.

> _____ _____ is a big problem all over the world. People cannot make quick decisions _____ _____ _____ when they drink alcohol. They are dangerous to themselves and _____ _____ _____ on the road. People are not keeping quiet about drunk driving anymore.

Basic Drills 2

Taking Notes: **Signal Words (II) - 표시어**

1. Signal words for addition
   : one more, furthermore, in addition, moreover, also, thus

2. Signal words for cause and effect
   : therefore, as a result, if ... then, so

On Your Own]

1. Read the passage and underline the signal words or phrases.

   > We must remember the three rules of soccer. First, we must not touch the ball with our hands. Second, the ball must not go out of the white line. Third, we must start in the middle of the field after we score a goal.

2. Listen carefully and write down all the signal words that you hear. MP3 89

   _____

   _____

3. Listen again and write your notes by using the signal words, symbols, abbreviations, and key words if necessary. MP3 90

Chapter 8. Social Issues

Listening Practice 1

MP3 91

Listen and choose the correct answer. As you listen, try to catch the hidden information.

People around the world always look for ~~~~~~~~~~.
~~~~~~~~~ all the time is ~~~~~~~~~~. There are ~~~~~
~~~~~~~~~~.
We must always remember ~~~~~~~~~~~~~ in life. ~~~~~~~~
~~~~ in the world is ~~~~~~, so we must be careful ~~~~~~~~. Paper
and tissue ~~~~~~~, and we should make sure ~~~~~~~~.
~~~~~~~~~~~~. Thanks to new technology, we can ~~~~~~
~~~~ in our daily lives. ~~~~~~~~~ are the most used items in the
world, and we can ~~~~~~~~. We should always remember ~~~~~~~
~~~~~~.

1 What is the passage mainly about?

 (A) Saving water
 (B) Reusing plastic items
 (C) Wasting the environment
 (D) Saving the environment

2 Why does the speaker mention water?

 (A) To describe a way of saving water
 (B) To give an example of what should not be wasted
 (C) To list all the different drinks of the world
 (D) To emphasize that we should reuse water

Listening Practice 2

Listen and choose the correct answer. As you listen, try to catch the hidden information.

W: Don't you think that ~~~~~~~~ on the streets? I can't get ~~~~~~~~.

M: I think it's great that ~~~~~~~~. You should use ~~~~~~~~. Public transportation seems ~~~~~~~~, if you want ~~~~~~~~.

W: ~~~~~~~~ when I'm traveling, and I can't seem ~~~~~~~~. I'm always ~~~~~~~~. It's the same in the subway as well. ~~~~~~~~ in subways.

M: Yes, it's ~~~~~~~~, but you had better ~~~~~~~~. It's much ~~~~~~~~ as well. You don't even ~~~~~~~~.

W: Yes, ~~~~~~~~. I guess I'll start ~~~~~~~~.

1 How does the man talk about public transportation?

(A) He emphasizes that cars are better.
(B) He lists where buses and subways stop.
(C) He compares it with driving cars.
(D) He gives examples of ways to travel.

2 Listen again to part of the conversation. Then answer the question. Why does the woman say this: 🎧

(A) To express a different idea
(B) To agree with the man
(C) To go and park the car with the man
(D) To take the bus with the man

Listening Practice 3

Listen and choose the correct answer.

MP3 93

Note-taking

1 What is the talk mainly about?

(A) Different ways of volunteering
(B) Similar ways of volunteering
(C) Methods of saving the highways
(D) Ways of donating blood

2 Listen again to part of the talk. Then answer the question. Why does the man say this: 🎧

(A) To say that the person will sleep
(B) To say that it is tiring to give blood
(C) To say that it is not hard to give blood
(D) To say that it is hard to give blood

Listening Practice 4

Listen and choose the correct answer.

MP3 94

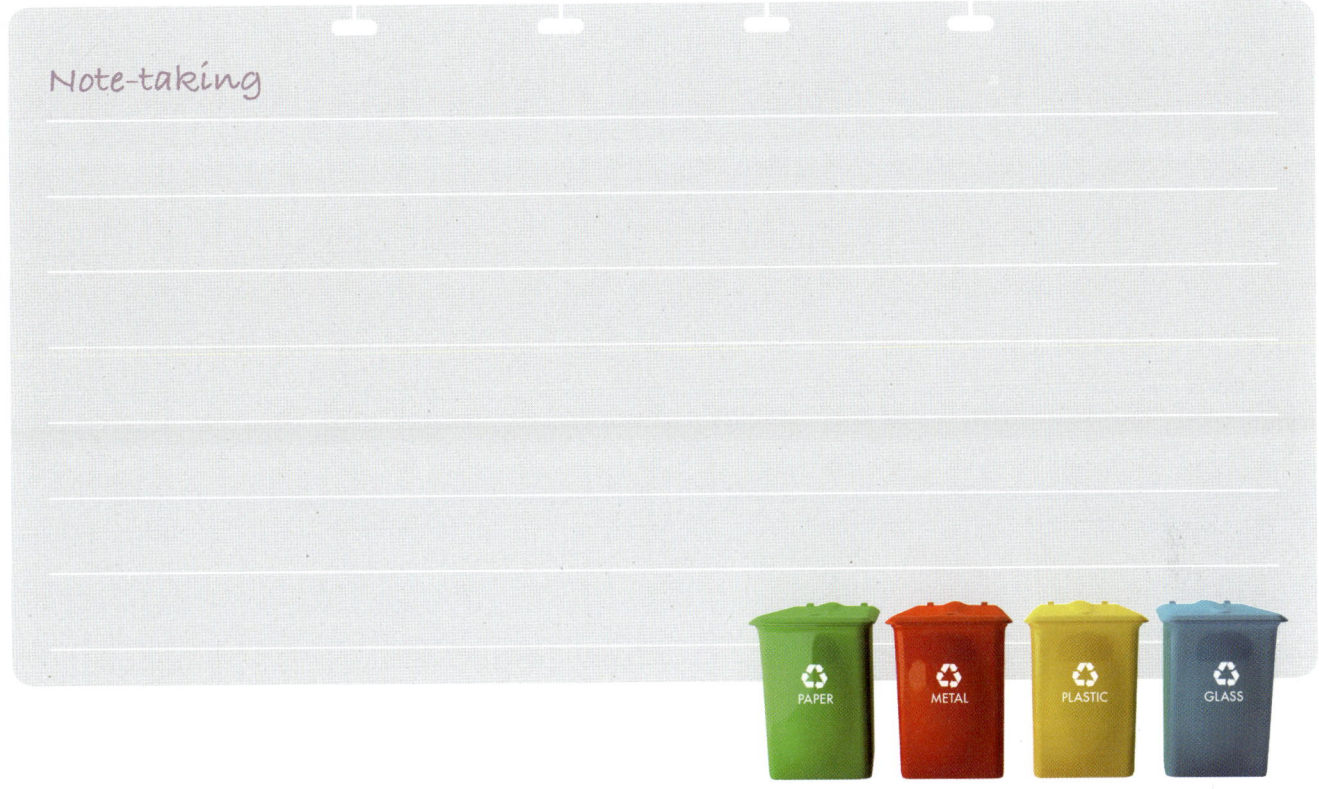

Note-taking

1 What is the man's attitude toward recycling?

(A) He does not think that recycling is important.
(B) He feels that recycling really helps the environment.
(C) He thinks that the woman should not recycle.
(D) He is not sure if he should recycle.

2 Listen again to part of the talk. Then answer the question.
Why does the man say this: 🎧

(A) To mention other ways to recycle
(B) To list other choices in recycling
(C) To emphasize that recycling is a waste of time
(D) To encourage the woman to continue recycling

Chapter 8. Social Issues **157**

Listening Practice 5

Listen and choose the correct answer.

Note-taking

1 How does the speaker talk about overseas education?

(A) He mentions the names of schools.
(B) He lists different countries that students go to study in.
(C) He gives examples of whom the students stay with.
(D) He gives examples of students in the schools.

2 Why does the speaker say that many students do not like boarding schools at first?

(A) To emphasize that boarding schools are bad
(B) To imply that most students like boarding schools after some time
(C) To say that he does not like boarding schools
(D) To indicate that boarding schools are better than normal schools

Listening Practice 6

Listen and choose the correct answer.

Note-taking

1. What is the man's attitude toward smoking?

   (A) He does not like smoking.
   (B) He is not sure if he likes smoking.
   (C) He likes smoking very much.
   (D) He is sure smoking is good.

2. Listen again to part of the conversation. Then answer the question. Why does the woman say this: 🎧

   (A) To list the different types of cigarettes
   (B) To give examples of other cigarettes
   (C) To show she had misunderstood the cause
   (D) To mention the ingredients in the cigarettes

Chapter 8. Social Issues

*i*BT Practice 1

TOEFL Listening

1 What is the conversation mainly about?

    Ⓐ Different culture systems in two countries
    Ⓑ Similar culture systems in two countries
    Ⓒ Different pots in two countries
    Ⓓ Different salads in two countries

2 According to the conversation, which of the following are true about the two systems? Tick in 2 answers.

    Ⓐ The melting pot system is used in the US.
    Ⓑ Canada does not mix cultures together.
    Ⓒ The Canadian system wants people to keep their culture.
    Ⓓ The melting pot system is better than the salad bowl toss system.

TOEFL Listening

Note-taking

3   Listen again to part of the conversation. Then answer the question.
    Why does the woman say this:

    Ⓐ To discourage the man
    Ⓑ To end the conversation
    Ⓒ To list her choice
    Ⓓ To give an idea for his writing

iBT Practice 2

TOEFL Listening

1 What is the talk mainly about?

- Ⓐ The World Wildlife Fund
- Ⓑ The International Red Cross
- Ⓒ Helping animals and plants
- Ⓓ Non-profit organizations

2 Listen again to part of the talk. Then answer the question. Why does the speaker say this: 🎧

- Ⓐ To express that the organization is always busy
- Ⓑ To indicate that they have a lot of free time
- Ⓒ To emphasize that they collect blood
- Ⓓ To say that organizations have no imagination

TOEFL Listening

Note-taking

3 What does the speaker mean when he says this: 🎧

Ⓐ He wants the organizations to stop helping people.
Ⓑ He wants more people to help in organizations.
Ⓒ He wants the world to be an organization.
Ⓓ He wants people to help only important organizations.

Dictation

iBT Practice 1

Listen and fill in the blanks. MP3 97

M: I have to _____ _____ _____ about a country's culture.

W: Really? _____ _____ are you going to write about?

M: I'm deciding on _____ _____ _____ on Canada or the US. _____ _____ _____ they have very different systems of _____ _____.

W: What do you mean? Aren't the two countries _____ _____ _____?

M: Yes, the two countries are close, but very different in _____ _____ _____. The US believes in a system called the "_____ _____."

W: Does that mean that they melt the cultures or _____ _____ _____?

M: I guess you _____ _____ _____. The US wants everyone to mix and create _____ _____ _____. That's to say, the Americans think that it will _____ _____ _____ together, and everyone will have _____ _____ _____ as others.

W: How about Canada? Do they _____ _____ _____?

M: Yes, Canada also mixes cultures together, but they call their system the "_____ _____ _____." They do not want people in their country to _____ _____ _____. Canadians think that _____ _____ _____ all the different cultures in the country.

W: Wow, both of them _____ _____. I guess it will be hard to say _____ _____ _____ correct. Sorry, but I have to go. I hope you make _____ _____ _____.

iBT Practice 2

Listen and fill in the blanks. MP3 98

_____ _____ help people without _____ _____ _____ at all. All the members and companies _____ _____ these organizations are volunteers. Some even use _____ _____ _____ when working in these organizations. There are _____ _____ _____ non-profit organizations.

　An example of _____ _____ _____ that helps other people is the International Red Cross. The International Red Cross _____ _____ _____ many things. They are like _____ _____ _____, with many doctors and nurses. The organization helps countries around the world _____ _____. They provide _____ _____ _____ in these countries. They also _____ _____ during their free time, although it is _____ _____ _____ that they have any free time at all.

　Non-profit organizations can also help _____ _____ _____. There is an organization called Greenpeace that works to _____ _____ _____. Another non-profit organization called the World Wildlife Fund protects animals _____ _____ _____. Both these organizations have _____ _____ _____ all over the world, and everyone in these organizations _____ _____ _____.

　_____ _____ _____ kind of organization, the most important part is _____ _____ that help others. Therefore, if all of us _____ _____ _____, the world will certainly become _____ _____ _____.

Word Review

Match the words from the box with the definitions.

| volunteer | donate | recycle | overseas |
| independence | destroy | emergency | shelter |

1 _____ across the ocean from your country

2 _____ to damage something so badly that it cannot be repaired

3 _____ someone who does work willingly, without being paid

4 _____ a place where you are protected from bad weather or danger

5 _____ to use something again, often for a different purpose

6 _____ to give something to a person or an organization in order to help them

7 _____ an unexpected and dangerous situation where immediate action is necessary

8 _____ the ability to make your own decisions in life without other people's help

Choose the best phrase to fit in each one of the blanks.

| throw away | on time | is responsible for | are involved in |

9 How many restaurants _____ the international food festival this year?

10 People in this town _____ thousands of tons of garbage every year.

11 Because the train always arrived _____ , people could set their watches by it.

12 Our department _____ preparing and carrying out advertising for the company.

useful **Phrasal Verbs**

+ **stand by** 지지하다
The students **stood by** each other before going on stage.

+ **stand for** 의미하다
What do the letters UNESCO **stand for**?

+ **suffer from** ~으로 고생하다
It was terrible that he **suffered from** the illness.

+ **sum up** 합하다
We should **sum up** the speech and get to the next level.

+ **take off** 벗다
Many Asian families **take off** their shoes before entering a home.

+ **talk over** 의논하다
You'd better **talk** it **over** with your teacher before you decide.

+ **turn down** 거절하다
They offered her a membership, but she **turned** it **down**.

+ **turn in** 돌려주다
The security guard **turned in** his keys before going home.

+ **turn up** 올리다
The party was dull, so they **turned up** the music.

+ **watch over** 지켜보다
The principal of the school **watched over** the children from his office.

+ **work out** 문제를 풀다, 해결하다
It is impossible to **work out** the puzzle within 10 minutes.

Mini Test
1 - 3

Mini Test 1

[MP3 99]

TOEFL Listening

1. What is the conversation mainly about?
   - A. Size of clocks
   - B. History of clocks
   - C. Shape of clocks
   - D. Carrying of clocks

2. According to the conversation, what did people use 100 years ago to tell time?
   - A. The sundial
   - B. The mechanical clock
   - C. The pocket watch
   - D. The wrist watch

3. What comparison is made between pocket watches and wrist watches?
   - A. The size of the watch
   - B. The working of the watch
   - C. The users of the watch
   - D. The function of the watch

4. Listen again to part of the conversation. Then answer the question. Why does the man say this:
   - A. To say that he uses the sundial
   - B. To say that he is sure of the sundial
   - C. To mention that he is not sure about the time
   - D. To encourage the woman to explain about the sundial

Mini Test 1

TOEFL Listening

5 According to the talk, who is Odysseus?

- Ⓐ He was one of the Trojans.
- Ⓑ He was the main character in *The Odyssey*.
- Ⓒ He wrote *The Odyssey* and *The Iliad*.
- Ⓓ He gave the Trojan horse to Cyclops.

6 Why does the speaker mention Cyclops?

- Ⓐ To give an example of a character in *The Odyssey*
- Ⓑ To give an example of a character in *The Iliad*
- Ⓒ To list the people in the Trojan horse
- Ⓓ To mention the author of the two stories

7 In what order does the speaker talk about Homer's poems?

- Ⓐ By the longer story to the shorter story
- Ⓑ By the time order of the story
- Ⓒ By the most important story to the least important story
- Ⓓ By the best story to the worst story

8 What is the speaker's attitude toward Homer and his poems?

- Ⓐ She thinks that Homer's poems are boring.
- Ⓑ She thinks that Homer's poems are too old.
- Ⓒ She thinks that Homer was a great man.
- Ⓓ She thinks that Homer was not special.

Mini Test 1

TOEFL Listening

TOEFL Listening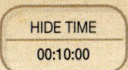

9 According to the discussion, which of the following are true about tough animals? Tick in the correct box.

	Yes	No
Ⓐ Camels do not drink water.		
Ⓑ Cockroaches are tough insects.		
Ⓒ Scorpions can live even when frozen in ice.		
Ⓓ Cockroaches can live without food for a year.		

10 Why does the teacher mention cockroaches?

Ⓐ To give an example of a tough insect
Ⓑ To agree with the woman about camels
Ⓒ To contrast with the scorpions
Ⓓ To list all the toughest animals

11 How does the teacher talk about scorpions?

Ⓐ He contrasts them with other animals.
Ⓑ He mentions what scorpions can endure.
Ⓒ He mentions what scorpions eat.
Ⓓ He identifies other tough insects.

12 Listen again to part of the discussion. Then answer the question. What does the woman mean when she says this: 🎧

Ⓐ She agrees with the teacher.
Ⓑ She is not sure about the answer.
Ⓒ She cannot beat the ice.
Ⓓ She wants to beat a scorpion.

Mini Test 2

TOEFL Listening

1 Why does the man talk to the librarian?

- Ⓐ To find his name on the computer
- Ⓑ To look for a book called *The Pearl* in the library
- Ⓒ To ask about the fine for a book he hasn't returned
- Ⓓ To inform the librarian that the book label is torn

2 Why does the woman say that many people make the same mistake?

- Ⓐ To warn the man that the problem is serious
- Ⓑ To list the problems that the man has caused
- Ⓒ To indicate that the mistake is not common
- Ⓓ To assure the man that it is not a big problem

3 How long has the man had the book?

- Ⓐ Over 3 months
- Ⓑ About 1 or 2 months
- Ⓒ About 10 months
- Ⓓ Over 4 months

4 Listen again to part of the conversation. Then answer the question. What does the man mean when he says this: 🎧

- Ⓐ He thinks that the fine is higher than he thought.
- Ⓑ He thinks that he should not pay the money.
- Ⓒ He thinks that the book is too expensive.
- Ⓓ He thinks that the fine is lower than he thought.

Mini Test 2

TOEFL Listening

5 What is the talk mainly about?

- A People enjoying musical instrumentsc
- B Things to make noise with
- C Countries without musical instruments
- D Music without musical instruments

6 According to the talk, what do people use to make music in "Nanta"?

- A They use things around our homes.
- B They only use knives on cutting boards.
- C They only use their voices to make music.
- D They use organs in churches of Italy.

7 How does the teacher talk about music?

- A By mentioning how people listen to music
- B By listing different types of music
- C By giving examples of when they perform
- D By contrasting between "Nanta" and "a capella"

8 What does the teacher mean when he says this:

- A "A capella" is a very easy type of music.
- B "A capella" singers practice around the world.
- C "A capella" is not an easy type of music.
- D "A capella" is not popular in some countries.

Mini Test 2

TOEFL Listening

TOEFL Listening

9 Why does the woman say it is stressful to choose clothes?

    Ⓐ To mention a good point about uniforms
    Ⓑ To indicate that uniforms are bad
    Ⓒ To give an example of her daily routine
    Ⓓ To change to another discussion topic

10 According to the discussion, what are the reasons schools make students wear uniforms? Tick in 2 answers.

    Ⓐ Uniforms stop students from wasting time on clothes.
    Ⓑ Uniforms stop students from showing off with expensive clothes.
    Ⓒ Uniforms are cheaper than other clothes.
    Ⓓ Uniform designs fit all students in schools.

11 What does the man imply about the students wearing school uniforms?

    Ⓐ He thinks that everyone must wear uniforms.
    Ⓑ He agrees that school uniforms can be a good idea.
    Ⓒ He thinks that school uniforms are helpful to students.
    Ⓓ He does not like school uniforms.

12 Listen again to part of the discussion. Then answer the question. Why does the man say this: 🎧

    Ⓐ To say that he thinks the woman is right
    Ⓑ To say that he still does not like wearing uniforms
    Ⓒ To make a point about wearing uniforms
    Ⓓ To correct the woman about the uniforms

Mini Test 3

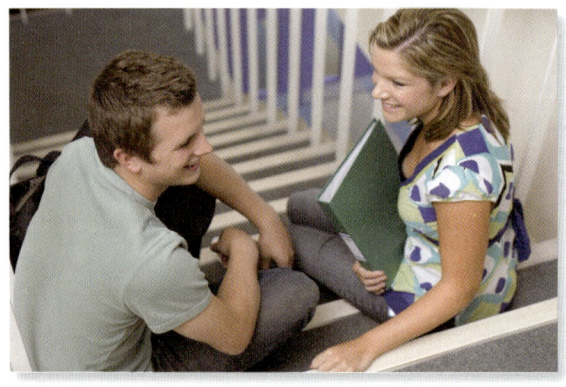

1 What is the conversation mainly about?

　Ⓐ Visiting old war buildings
　Ⓑ Traveling to a foreign country
　Ⓒ Eating in a romantic restaurant
　Ⓓ Places to visit in Paris

2 According to the conversation, what can the man do in Paris? Tick in the correct box.

	Yes	No
Ⓐ Eat on the top floor of the Eiffel Tower		
Ⓑ Eat on the top floor of the Arc de Triomphe		
Ⓒ Walk inside the Arc de Triomphe		
Ⓓ See Napoleon's name on the wall		

3 What does the woman compare between Paris and other cities around the world?

　Ⓐ How many restaurants there are
　Ⓑ How many buildings there are
　Ⓒ How many buildings there are
　Ⓓ How brave the soldiers are

4 What can be inferred about the woman?

　Ⓐ She comes from Paris.
　Ⓑ She thinks that Paris is an attractive city.
　Ⓒ She did not enjoy the trip to Paris.
　Ⓓ She has never been to Paris.

Mini Test 3

TOEFL Listening

TOEFL Listening

5 What is the talk mainly about?
- Ⓐ The structure of frog eggs
- Ⓑ The life cycle of frogs
- Ⓒ Tadpoles in water
- Ⓓ Gills and lungs

6 According to the teacher, what are true about frogs and tadpoles? Tick in the correct box.

	Yes	No
Ⓐ Adult frogs lay eggs in the water.		
Ⓑ Tadpoles use gills to breathe.		
Ⓒ Tadpoles have eyes when inside the eggs.		
Ⓓ Adult frogs use gills to breathe.		

7 In what order does the speaker talk about frogs?
- Ⓐ From eggs to adult frogs
- Ⓑ From young frogs to tadpoles
- Ⓒ From tadpoles to tadpoles with legs
- Ⓓ From growing a tail to growing legs

8 What can be inferred about tadpoles?
- Ⓐ They cannot look for food on their own.
- Ⓑ They can live both in and out of water.
- Ⓒ Their hands grow first, and then their legs.
- Ⓓ Their gills disappear when they are about 3 months old.

Mini Test 3

TOEFL Listening

TOEFL Listening

9 What is the discussion mainly about?
- Ⓐ The oldest drawing
- Ⓑ The earliest sport
- Ⓒ The rules of wrestling
- Ⓓ The fun of sports

10 What was found on the cave walls?
- Ⓐ Paintings of animals
- Ⓑ List of rules on wrestling
- Ⓒ Paintings of people wrestling
- Ⓓ Paintings of people running

11 According to the discussion, what is the meaning of sports?
- Ⓐ Exercise to hunt or run away
- Ⓑ Exercise that is forced by someone
- Ⓒ Exercise that is done for fun
- Ⓓ Exercise to be healthy

12 Listen again to part of the discussion. Then answer the question. Why does the man say this: 🎧
- Ⓐ To express his agreement with her opinion
- Ⓑ To indicate that her argument does not make sense
- Ⓒ To let her give some more details
- Ⓓ To move on to the next topic

Final iBT

http://www.finalibt.co.kr

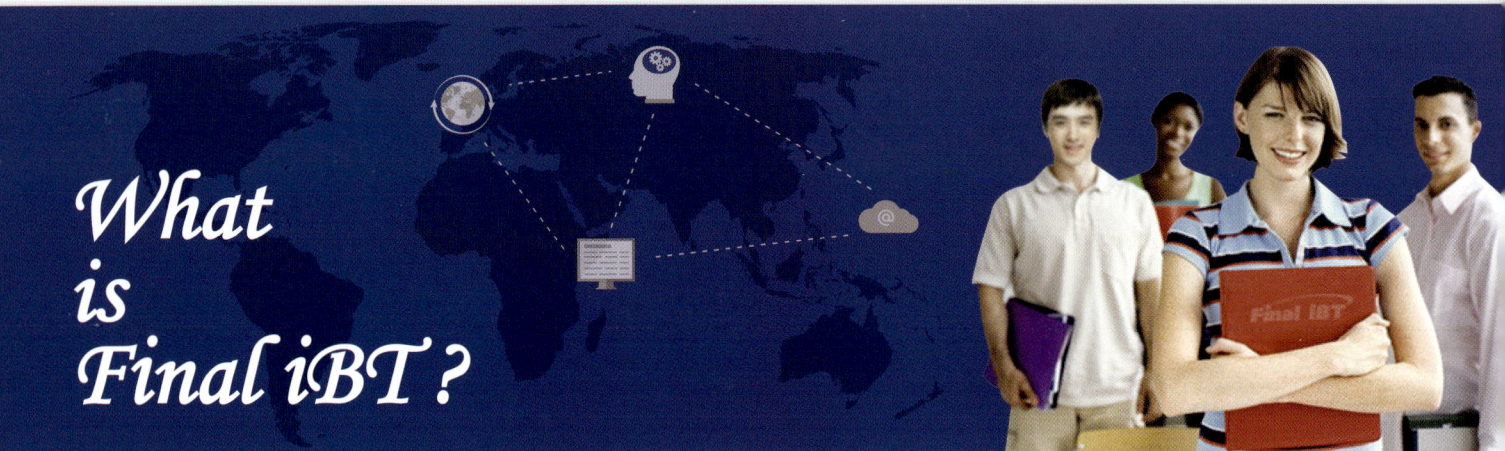

What is Final iBT?

Final iBT는 TOEFL 시험을 준비하는 학습자를 위한 완벽한 준비 도구로서 실제 IBT시험을 치르는 것과 같은 full-length의 연습테스트를 제공합니다. 지난 시험들을 통해 철저히 분석된 문제들을 연습하게 되며 48시간 이내에 점수를 받아볼 수 있습니다.

시험을 마친 후 상세한 그래프와 함께 자신의 점수를 분석할 수 있습니다. 또한 자신이 풀었던 문제와 답뿐만 아니라 Reading, Listening, Speaking, Writing의 스크립트를 제공받아 철저한 복습이 가능합니다.
Final iBT는 토플 모의 시험으로써 토플 준비를 위한 완벽한 학습 자료가 될 것입니다.

시험 구성

: 시험 구성은 다음과 같습니다.

Level	Test Version	Questions (문항)			
		Reading	Listening	Speaking	Writing
고급	Full	39~42	34	6	2
	Short	14~28	17	3	1
	Half (R/L)	39~42	34	X	X
	Half (S/W)	X	X	6	2
초급	Short	21~24	13	2	1

* 총 40회분의 시험이 제공됩니다.

http://www.finalibt.co.kr

PERFECT SOLUTION for **TOEFL Junior**

*i*BT **NEW EDITION**

b TOEFL LISTENING

Scripts & Answer Key

MP3파일 무료제공 http://test.linguaforum.com

LinguaForum

Scripts & Answer Key

LinguaForum

Chapter 1
History
/ Main Idea

Overview p.11

Sample Question: (C)

Basic Drills 1 p.12

1. (C)   2. (A)

1. W: What's wrong? You look worried.
   M: I am confused. I need to know when the Second World War was over.
   W: Really? Wasn't that in 1942? Wait, now I am confused. Was it 1943?
   M: No, I don't think so. I think it's either 1944 or 1945.
   W: 무슨 일이니? 고민 있나 보네.
   M: 헷갈리는 게 있어서. 2차 세계 대전이 언제 끝났는지 알아야겠는데.
   W: 정말? 그거 1942년 아니었니? 잠깐, 이제 나도 헷갈린다. 1943년이었나?
   M: 아니, 아닌 것 같아. 1944년 아니면 1945년 둘 중에 하나야.

2. The earliest postmen rode on horses. The post offices were called the Pony Express. People would ride their horses with mailbags. There would be stations every 30 kilometers to change horses. Each rider rode for about 160 to 200 kilometers each time they made delivery. The brave riders rode their horses no matter what the weather was like.
   초기 우체부들은 말을 탔었다. 사람들은 우체국을 조랑말 속달 우편(Pony Express)이라고 불렀다. 우체부들은 우편가방을 들고 말을 탔다. 30킬로미터마다 말을 갈아타기 위한 정류장이 있었다. 한 사람의 우체부가 배달하러 갈때마다 보통 160에서 200킬로미터를 달렸다. 그 용감한 우체부들은 날씨가 어떻든 상관하지 않고 말을 달렸다.

Basic Drills 2 p.13

On Your Own

Possible Answer

1. (1) The law is fair to everyone. / The law is equal for everyone.
   (2) Kay's house is larger (or bigger) than my uncle's.
2. (1) Sue > Betty, Sue pants = Betty
   (2) royal England ≠ royal China

2. (1) Sue is taller than Betty, but they wear the same size pants.
   (2) The royal family in England did not live like the royal family in China.

Listenining Practice ❶ p.14

1. (D)   2. (B)

Chinese characters are very hard to learn. Long ago, Koreans only had Chinese characters as their written language. However, King Sejong changed all that.

King Sejong realized that there were many problems because common people could not read or write the Chinese characters. Only scholars and noblemen knew how to read. King Sejong wanted to help his people understand a written language. He called the smartest scholars of Korea to start developing a new written language for Koreans.

After many years, King Sejong declared that "Hangul" was born. Many Koreans were very happy with the new language. Hangul was much easier to learn than Chinese characters. King Sejong is still remembered today as a very wise king.

한자는 배우기가 아주 어렵다. 오래 전, 한국 사람들은 문자로 한자만을 썼었다. 그러나 세종대왕은 그것들을 모두 바꿔 놓

앉다.
　세종대왕은 백성들이 한자를 읽고 쓰지 못해서 많은 문제가 발생한다는 것을 알게 되었다. 오직 학자들과 양반만이 글을 읽을 줄 알았다. 세종대왕은 그의 백성들이 글을 알 수 있도록 돕고 싶었다. 그는 나라에서 가장 현명한 학자들을 불러 한국 사람들을 위한 글자를 개발하기 시작했다.
　수년 후, 세종대왕은 '한글'이 창제되었음을 알렸다. 많은 한국 사람들은 새로운 언어에 매우 기뻐했다. 한글은 한자보다 훨씬 배우기가 쉬웠다. 세종대왕은 오늘날까지 아주 현명한 왕으로 기억되고 있다.

Listenining Practice ❷　p.15

1. (B)　2. (C)

　The *Titanic* was one of the largest ships in the world. It was also one of the most luxurious. There were over 2,000 people on the ship. The engineers were very sure that the *Titanic* would not sink, so there were only a few lifeboats.
　Unfortunately, the *Titanic* did sink. The ship hit an iceberg and sank slowly. The lifeboats could not take everyone on the ship. Some lifeboats even sailed off before they were full of passengers.
　The people who could not get on the lifeboats fell into the water. The water was very cold, and many people froze to death. Other ships were far away, so they could not come to save them. Almost 1,500 people died when the *Titanic* sank.
　타이타닉호는 세계에서 가장 큰 배중 하나였다. 또한 가장 호화로운 배중 하나이기도 했다. 배에는 2천명이 탑승했다. 기술자들은 타이타닉이 침몰하지 않을 것이라고 확신했기 때문에 배에는 구명보트 몇 정만이 있었다.
　불행하게도 타이타닉은 침몰했다. 그 배는 빙산과 충돌하여 서서히 가라앉았다. 구명보트는 그 배에 탄 모든 사람들을 실을 수 없었다. 몇몇 구명보트들은 정원이 다 차기도 전에 출발해버렸다.
　구명보트에 타지 못한 사람들은 물에 빠졌다. 물은 아주 차가웠고 많은 사람들이 얼어 죽었다. 다른 배들은 너무 멀리 떨어져있어서 그들을 구하러 올 수 없었다. 타이타닉의 침몰로 약 1,500명의 사람들이 죽었다.

Listenining Practice ❸　p.16

1. (A)　2. (B)

　Venice was an important city for Europe during the 11th century. Venice port was full of merchants, who shared information about other countries. It was in Venice that Marco Polo became a merchant.
　When Marco was 21, he and his father sailed off to China. They were the first Europeans to go to many parts of China. There was much to learn about China because it was the most developed country at that time. They saw many things that Europeans did not know about. Marco was even the first European to see the Great Wall.
　Marco came back to Venice in 1292 and shared information about China with the Europeans. Many people still remember him as a great merchant.
　베니스는 11세기 유럽에서 중요한 도시였다. 베니스 항은 다른 나라에 대한 정보를 공유하는 상인들로 가득했다. 마르코 폴로가 상인이 된 곳도 베니스였다.
　마르코가 21살이었을 때 그와 그의 아버지는 중국으로 항해를 떠났다. 그들은 중국의 많은 지방을 다닌 최초의 유럽인들이었다. 중국은 그 당시에 가장 발전된 국가였기 때문에 배울 것들이 많이 있었다. 그들은 유럽인들이 알지 못했던 많은 것들을 보게 되었다. 마르코는 만리장성을 본 최초의 유럽인이었다.
　마르코는 1292년 베니스로 돌아와 유럽사람들에게 중국에 대한 소식을 알려주었다. 많은 사람들은 아직도 그를 위대한 상인으로 기억한다.

Listenining Practice ❹　p.17

1. (D)　2. (C)

T: We're going to talk about the black leaders of America. Does anyone know of any black leaders?
M: I heard of Malcolm X, who led black people in the fight for freedom.
W: There was also Martin Luther King Jr., who believed in peace.
T: Yes, Malcolm X and Martin Luther King were both famous black leaders of America. Who do

you think was correct?
M: I think Malcolm was correct to fight.
W: Are you sure about that? I think that King was correct to have peaceful protests. He even received the Nobel Peace Prize.
M: I still don't think he achieved as much as Malcolm. Not fighting means giving up.
W: That isn't true. Fighting only makes people angrier.
T: Both were great leaders and believed in different things. Because of them, the world is now a better place to live for everyone.

T: 미국의 흑인 지도자들에 대해서 공부해보자. 혹시 알고 있는 흑인 지도자가 있니?
M: 말콤 X에 대해 들어봤어요. 그는 흑인들이 자유를 위해 투쟁하도록 이끌었어요.
W: 마틴 루터 킹 2세도 있어요. 그는 평화를 신봉했어요.
T: 그래, 말콤 X와 마틴 루터 킹은 둘 다 유명한 미국의 흑인 지도자들이다. 너희들 생각에는 누가 옳은 것 같니?
M: 제 생각에는 말콤 X의 투쟁 방법이 옳은 것 같아요.
W: 정말 그렇게 생각하니? 내 생각에는 평화롭게 저항한 마틴 루터 킹이 옳은 것 같아. 그 사람은 노벨 평화상까지 받았는걸.
M: 그래도 나는 그가 말콤만큼 많은 성과를 이루지 못했다고 생각해. 싸우지 않는다는 것은 포기하는 거잖아.
W: 그렇지 않아. 싸움은 사람들을 더 성나게 만들 뿐이야.
T: 둘 다 위대한 지도자들이었고, 단지 다른 가치관을 가졌던 사람들이란다. 그 두 사람 덕택에 세상은 모두가 살기에 더 좋아졌단다.

Listenining Practice ❺ p.18

1. (B)   2. (A)

Ever since Adam and Eve, men and women have been treated differently. Men have been in control of many parts of life over women for many years. It was thought long ago that women were weaker and didn't know how to work. Some countries still treat men and women differently.

In some Middle Eastern countries, women are not allowed to study or work. It is illegal for them to even drive or play sports. The law also says that women cannot wear certain clothes. Nevertheless, some of these countries are slowly changing the laws to be fairer to women.

Today, it is illegal in most countries to treat men and women differently. We must realize that men and women are equal and can do the same things.

아담과 이브 때부터 남자와 여자는 다른 대우를 받았다. 남자는 오랜 동안 여자보다 생활의 많은 부분에서 주도권을 갖고 있었다. 옛날에는 여자는 약해서 일을 할 줄 모른다고 인식되었었다. 어떤 나라에서는 아직도 남자와 여자를 다르게 대한다.

몇몇 중동 국가에서는 여자가 공부나 일을 하는 것이 허용되지 않는다. 여자들이 운전을 하거나 운동을 하는 것 조차 불법이다. 또한 법에는 여자는 특정한 옷을 입어서는 안된다고 명시되어 있다. 그럼에도 불구하고, 몇몇 나라에서는 여자에게 좀 더 공정한 쪽으로 서서히 법이 바뀌고 있다.

오늘날 대부분의 나라에서는 남자와 여자를 다르게 대우하는 것이 불법이다. 우리는 남자와 여자는 동등하고 같은 일을 할 수 있다는 것을 깨달아야 한다.

Listenining Practice ❻ p.19

1. (D)   2. (B)

M: I was absent yesterday. What did the teacher talk about in history class?
W: The gold rush in America. Do you know anything about it?
M: No, I don't. Was it in New York?
W: No, it was in California. Some people were building a wood factory when they saw gold in 1848.
M: Wow, really? Did many people know about the gold after that?
W: Yes, many heard that there was a lot of gold and went to California to become rich. Within 5 years, there were 250,000 people in the gold fields.
M: Did all of them get rich?
W: No, they did not. In fact, a lot of people suffered and died, as they were not prepared for the long journey.
M: You're kidding. That is a sad story. Were there other large gold rushes?

W: Not in the US. There were a few large gold rushes in Canada, though.
M: 나 어제 결석했어. 선생님께서 역사 시간에 무슨 얘기 하셨니?
W: 미국의 골드러시에 대해서 말씀하셨어. 골드러시에 대해서 아니?
M: 아니 몰라. 뉴욕에서 있던 일이야?
W: 아니 캘리포니아에서 있던 일이야. 1848년도에 사람들이 제재소를 만들때 금을 발견한 거야.
M: 와, 정말? 그러고 나서 많은 사람들이 금에 대해 알게 된 거야?
W: 응, 거기에 금이 많이 있다는 걸 듣고 많은 사람들이 부자가 되겠다면서 캘리포니아로 갔어. 5년 동안 금광지대에는 25만 명이 모였어.
M: 다들 부자가 됐니?
W: 아니, 못됐어. 사실 많은 사람들이 긴 여정을 대비하지 못해서 고생하다 죽었어.
M: 말도 안돼. 슬픈 얘기다. 또 다른 큰 골드러시도 있었니?
W: 미국에선 없었어. 캐나다에서 큰 골드러시가 좀 있었어.

iBT Practice 1 p.20

1. (B)   2. (D)   3. (C)

Listen to part of a talk in a history class.

The original Olympics were first held by the Greeks more than 2,500 years ago. It was a very big and popular event, but a Roman king stopped the games.

The first modern Olympic Games started again 1,500 years later. They were held in Athens in 1896. The games were to promote peace by using sports.

The first few Olympics were not very popular. The Olympics were not well-known, so the athletes were not properly trained. Some athletes of the first modern Olympics were tourists that were passing by the stadium.

Just as the games were getting popular, World War I broke out. Because of this, the games were not held. In fact, the modern games did not take place three times due to the World Wars.

Although the Olympics were not about money, host countries spent and lost a lot of money. This was why big companies were allowed to advertise in the event. This made the Olympics a much larger event than before.

첫 올림픽은 2,500년 이상 거슬러 올라가 그리스인들에 의해서 최초로 개최되었다. 올림픽은 아주 규모가 크고 인기 있는 행사였지만 로마의 왕이 경기를 중단시켰다.

최초의 근대 올림픽은 1,500년 뒤 다시 개최되었다. 올림픽은 1896년 아테네에서 개최되었다. 올림픽 경기는 스포츠를 통하여 평화를 증진시키기 위한 것이었다.

초기 몇 번의 올림픽은 별로 인기가 없었다. 올림픽은 잘 알려지지 않았고, 선수들이 제대로 훈련되지 못했다. 초창기 근대 올림픽에서는 경기장 옆을 지나치던 관광객들이 선수로 경기를 하기도 했었다.

경기가 인기를 얻게 되었을 때 1차 세계 대전이 발발했다. 이 때문에 올림픽은 개최되지 못했다. 사실 근대 올림픽은 세계 대전으로 인해 세 번이나 개최되지 못했다.

비록 돈 때문에 올림픽을 하는 것은 아니지만 개최국은 많은 돈을 지출하고 손해를 봤다. 그래서 대기업들이 올림픽 행사를 통해 광고를 하도록 허용하였다. 이것이 근대 올림픽이 이전보다 더 큰 행사가 되도록 만들었다.

iBT Practice 2 p.22

1. (A)   2. (D)   3. (C)

Listen to part of a talk in a history class.

During the early 1900s, blacks in America suffered a lot from white people. Blacks also had a very tough time from the government. Because of this, two famous black Americans started an organization called the Black Panthers.

The Black Panthers had guns and trained members to fight like soldiers. They trained to protect themselves. They told black people to stand up and fight. The Black Panthers also told other black Americans that they were equal to white Americans. The government did not like the group, and they did not want black Americans to have power.

The Black Panthers also helped the black society. Most blacks during that time were poor, so they opened kitchens to feed breakfast to over 10,000 children every day. They also had newspapers to share news about the black community.

The government did many things to try and stop the group. For instance, they tried to make the group confused by giving wrong information to other people. The government also had many famous black leaders killed.

1900년대 초반, 미국의 흑인들은 백인들 때문에 많은 고통을 받았다. 또 흑인들은 정부로 인해 부당한 나날을 보냈다. 이로 인해 두 명의 흑인이 블랙팬더라는 조직을 만들었다.

블랙팬더는 총을 가졌고 조직원들을 군인처럼 싸울 수 있도록 훈련시켰다. 그들은 자신들을 방어하기 위해 훈련했다. 그들은 흑인들에게 일어나 싸울 것을 요구했다. 블랙팬더는 다른 흑인들에게 그들은 백인들과 동등하다고 말했다. 정부는 그 조직을 좋아하지 않았고 흑인들이 힘을 갖도록 허락하지 않았다.

블랙팬더는 흑인 사회를 돕기도 했다. 그 당시 대부분의 흑인들은 가난했다. 그래서 그들은 식당을 열고 매일 만 명 이상의 아이들에게 아침 식사를 제공했다. 그들은 또 흑인 사회에 대한 소식들을 공유하기 위한 신문을 발행했다.

정부에서 그 조직을 막기 위해 많은 일을 시도했다. 예를 들어, 가짜 정보를 주어 조직에 혼란을 가져오게 하였고, 많은 유명한 흑인 지도자들을 죽이기도 했다.

Word Review p.26

1. sink	2. illegal
3. replace	4. merchant
5. feed	6. promote
7. luxurious	8. athlete
9. broke out	10. suffered from
11. No matter what	12. takes place

Chapter 2
Sports
/ Supporting Detail

Overview p.31

Sample Question: (B)

Basic Drills 1 p.32

1. (C)   2. (B)

1. Many new sports are created every day. Some can become very popular. Inline skating is such a sport. It was used mainly by ice hockey players who needed special skates to train in summer. The skates were very popular among younger people, and now, everyone likes inline skates.

매일 많은 새로운 경기들이 생겨난다. 어떤 것들은 큰 인기를 얻게 된다. 인라인 스케이트가 바로 그런 스포츠이다. 인라인 스케이트는 여름에 훈련을 하기 위해 특별한 스케이트가 필요했던 아이스 하키 선수들이 주로 사용하였다. 이 스케이트는 젊은이들 사이에서 아주 유명해져서 지금은 모든 사람들이 인라인 스케이트를 좋아한다.

2. W: Sports are fun and exciting. Everyone should play sports. Doctors say that we need the exercise to keep our bodies healthy.
   M: Really? Is that the only reason why we should play sports? I don't really care about health.
   W: Sports are also good for a healthy mind. They release stress, and you can also make more friends.

   W: 스포츠는 재미있고 흥미진진해. 모든 사람들이 운동을 해야 해. 의사들은 우리 몸을 건강하게 유지하려면 운동을 해야 한대.
   M: 정말? 그게 우리가 운동을 해야 하는 유일한 이유니? 난 건강에는 신경 안쓰는데.

W: 운동은 정신건강에도 좋아. 운동을 하면 스트레스도 줄고 친구들도 많이 사귈 수 있어.

Basic Drills 2 p.33

On Your Own

Possible Answer

1. (1) Regular exercise leads to a longer life.
   (2) Good manners come from good parenting.
2. (1) singers losing money ← internet
   (2) eating too much → many problems

2. (1) Singers are losing money because of the internet.
   (2) Eating too much can cause many problems.

Listenining Practice ❶ p.34

1. (B) 2. (C)

All students in schools study hard and learn new things. Some even go to institutes for further studies. There are some students that also study sports. In South America, there are many schools that teach children to be professional soccer players.

The children study the same things in school, but they must also learn and train in soccer. The graduates of the schools are respected by many people, and most become professional soccer players.

China is famous for diving. This is because children as little as 4 years old start training in diving schools. They eat and live in the school. They study the same things in school like other students, but they also train for more than 10 hours after school. They usually have a much harder life than students in other schools.

학교에 있는 모든 학생들은 수업시간에 열심히 공부를 하고 새로운 것들을 배운다. 어떤 학생들은 공부를 더 하기 위해 학원을 다니기도 한다. 어떤 학생들은 운동을 배우기도 한다.

남미에는 아이들에게 프로 축구 선수가 되도록 가르치는 학교가 많다. 아이들은 학교에서 똑같이 공부를 배우지만 그들은 축구도 배우고 훈련을 받는다. 그 학교의 졸업생들은 많은 사람들에게 인정을 받고, 그들 중 대부분은 프로 축구 선수가 된다.

중국은 다이빙으로 유명하다. 그 이유는 4살 정도의 어린 아이 때부터 다이빙 학교에서 훈련을 하기 때문이다. 그들은 학교에서 먹고 생활한다. 그들은 다른 학생들처럼 학교에서 수업을 받고 방과 후 10시간 이상을 훈련한다. 그들은 일반 학교의 학생들보다 더 힘든 생활을 한다.

Listenining Practice ❷ p.35

1. (C) 2. Yes: (B), (C) / No: (A), (D)

There are many different types of sports in the world. There are some popular sports like soccer and tennis, but they are not popular in Noth America. North Americans prefer to watch other kinds of sports, such as American football and ice hockey.

American football uses a ball that looks like a rugby ball. There are 11 players on each team, and all players wear special protective clothes. The most important player on the team is the quarterback. The quarterback throws the ball to a receiver or runner who catches the ball and runs to the goal area.

On the other hand, ice hockey is played by many Canadians and Americans. Ice hockey uses a flat puck as a ball. There are 6 players on each team. The players wear safety clothes and skates. They can only use their sticks to move the puck.

세상에는 여러 가지 종류의 스포츠가 있다. 축구나 테니스 같은 인기 있는 스포츠도 있지만 북미에서는 인기가 없다. 북미 사람들은 미식축구나 아이스하키같은 다른 종류의 스포츠 보는 것을 더 좋아한다.

미식축구에서는 럭비공처럼 생긴 공을 사용한다. 각 팀에 11명의 선수가 경기를 하고, 모든 선수들은 특수 보호 장치가 된 옷을 입는다. 팀에서 가장 중요한 선수는 쿼터백이다. 쿼터백은 공을 잡고 득점 지역까지 달리는 리시버나 러너에게 공을 던져준다.

반면, 아이스하키는 캐나다인들과 미국인들이 많이 하는 경기이다. 아이스하키는 납작한 퍽을 공으로 사용한다. 각 팀에는 여섯 명의 선수들이 있다. 선수들은 안전 장치가 된 옷을 착용하고 스케이트를 신는다. 퍽을 움직이려면 스틱 만을 사용할 수 있다.

Listenining Practice ❸ p.36

1. (B)   2. (A)

T: What do you think is a dangerous sport?
W: How about lacrosse? It's a game where each player has a stick with a net and tries to score a goal.
T: That's right. It's a tough and popular sport among high school and university students in the US. People get hurt often.
M: It seems like a dangerous game to me. I hope they wear protective clothing when they play.
W: Oh, yes. They wear a helmet, gloves and some shoulder pads.
T: Alright, how about the safest sport?
M: That's hard to say. People can get hurt in many ways. I remember one. How about lawn bowling?
W: That isn't even a sport. It's just some people rolling heavy balls on the grass.
T: Actually, it is a sport.
W: But the game is so slow. It would be hard for people to get hurt playing the game.

T: 위험한 운동으로는 어떤 것이 있을까?
W: 라크로스는 어때요? 각각의 선수가 그물이 달린 스틱을 들고 골을 넣는 경기에요.
T: 맞아. 미국에서 고등학교와 대학교 학생들 사이에서 인기있는 거친 스포츠이지. 종종 다치기도 한단다.
M: 내가 보기에는 위험한 경기 같은데. 경기할 때 보호 장비를 착용했으면 좋겠어요.
W: 그래, 선수들은 헬멧, 장갑, 그리고 어깨보호대를 착용해.
T: 좋아. 그럼 가장 안전한 경기는 뭐가 있을까?
M: 어렵네요. 사람들은 여러 가지 이유로 다칠 수 있잖아요. 하나 생각났어요. 잔디 볼링은 어때요?
W: 그건 스포츠도 아니야. 그건 그냥 몇몇 사람들이 잔디에서 무거운 공을 굴리는 거지.
T: 그래도 그것도 스포츠란다.
W: 하지만 경기가 아주 느리던데요. 사람들이 그 경기 하다가 다치는 게 더 어려울 거에요.

Listenining Practice ❹ p.37

1. (A)   2. (D)

A long time ago, there was no worldwide event for skaters and BMX riders. Then, a television channel called ESPN decided to make a sports show called the X Games.

The X Games was made for younger viewers. The Games first had skaters, BMX riders and inline skaters as athletes. The show immediately drew a lot of attention. More people wanted to be part of the games. Even people who did not skate or ride bicycles also enjoyed watching the show.

The X Games grew very quickly, and it was a favorite show among younger people all over the world. The show added more events, such as rock and ice climbing. The Winter X Games was also added to feature snowboarding and other winter events.

예전에는 스케이트 선수나 BMX 선수들을 위한 국제 경기가 없었다. 그래서 ESPN이라는 채널에서 X게임이라고 부르는 스포츠 프로그램을 만들었다.

X게임은 젊은 시청자들을 위해 만들어졌다. 처음에는 스케이트 선수, BMX 선수, 인라인 스케이트 선수들이 출연했다. 그 프로그램은 순식간에 큰 주목을 받았다. 더 많은 사람들이 게임에 참가하고 싶어했다. 스케이트나 자전거를 안 타는 사람들 까지도 그 프로를 즐기게 되었다.

X게임은 아주 빠르게 성장했고 전 세계 젊은이들이 가장 좋아하는 프로가 되었다. 그 프로그램은 암벽 등반, 빙벽 등반 등 많은 종목들을 더 추가했다. 스노우보딩이나 다른 동계 종목을 특색 있게 다루는 동계 X게임도 추가됐다.

Listenining Practice ❺ p.38

1. (C)   2. (B)

How many different sports are played in your country? Each country seems to have a special sport. Curling is a popular sport in Canada.

Curling is a group sport and is played on ice. Each team has 4 players. Each member has two tries to slide a "stone" close to a circle on the ice. The circle is about 50 meters away from the start line. The stones are round with a flat base and have a handle on top.

The team uses a brush to sweep the ice when the stone is sliding to the circle. They do this to make the ice smooth, so that the stone will not stop and go straight. The teams try to slide the stones to hit the other team's stones and push them away. The winner is the team with the stone that is closest to the center of the circle.

당신의 나라에는 얼마나 많은 종류의 스포츠가 있는가? 각 나라마다 특별한 운동 경기가 하나씩은 있는 듯 하다. 컬링은 캐나다에서 인기 있는 경기이다.

컬링은 단체 경기이며 빙상에서 하는 경기이다. 각 팀은 네 명으로 구성되어 있다. 팀의 각 선수들은 둥근 돌을 얼음 위의 원에 가깝도록 미끄러뜨리는 것을 두 번씩 한다. 그 원은 출발선에서 50미터 떨어져 있다. 돌은 둥글고 바닥은 납작하며 위쪽에는 손잡이가 달려있다.

돌이 원으로 미끄러지는 동안 팀원들은 브러시를 이용하여 얼음 바닥을 쓸어 준다. 이렇게 하는 것은 얼음을 부드럽게 하여 돌이 멈추지 않고 똑바로 가게 하기 위해서이다. 양팀은 돌을 미끄러뜨려서 상대팀의 돌을 맞춰 밀어낸다. 원의 중앙에 가까운 돌이 있는 팀이 이기게 된다.

Listenining Practice 🎧 p.39

1. (C) 2. (B)

Muhammad Ali was the best boxer in the world. He won a gold medal in the Olympics and had many championship belts. He was named Sportsman of the Century. Ali was famous not only for boxing, but also for other reasons.

Ali's original name was Cassius Clay. He changed his name to Muhammad Ali after changing to Islam. Islam is a religion from the Middle East. Many people were surprised and shocked at this news.

Ali also refused to join the war in Vietnam. Ali said he had no reason to fight the Vietnamese. The government said that he could go to jail and took his Olympic medal and belts away. After fighting in court, he did not have to go to jail and was allowed to box again.

무하마드 알리는 세계 최고의 복서이다. 그는 올림픽에서 금메달을 땄고 많은 챔피언 벨트를 가지고 있었다. 그는 세기의 스포츠맨이라고 불린다. 알리는 권투뿐 아니라 다른 이유로도 유명하다.

알리의 본명은 캐시우스 클레이다. 그는 이슬람교로 개종한 후에 무하마드 알리로 이름을 바꿨다. 이슬람교는 중동의 종교이다. 많은 사람들이 이 소식을 듣고 놀라고 충격을 받았다.

알리는 베트남전 참전도 거부했다. 알리는 베트남 사람들과 싸울 이유가 없다고 말했다. 정부는 그가 감옥에 갈 수 있고 올림픽 메달과 챔피언 벨트를 빼앗아 갈 수도 있다고 했다. 법정에서 싸우고 나서야 그는 감옥에 갈 필요도 없었고 다시 권투를 할 수 있게 되었다.

iBT Practice 1 p.40

1. (D)   2. (B)   3. (A)

Listen to part of a talk in school.

The X Games have shown many people that extreme sports can be fun and safe. Rock climbing is one of those sports. There are a few reasons why it is getting more popular.

Rock climbing is getting safer all the time. Companies are constantly making safer rock climbing gear. Long ago, the safety equipment in rock climbing was of very low quality, and it was not really safe to use it. These days, safety gear is strong enough to carry an elephant without breaking.

With better building materials, people have been able to develop real-looking indoor climbing walls. This allows beginners to practice safely, with proper coaching, at minimum risk. They can learn how to climb properly and be prepared for real climbing in the mountains.

Rock climbing has also been viewed as dangerous by many people due to old and wrong information. The internet has helped people better understand rock climbing. This has made more people interested in the sport.

X게임은 많은 사람들에게 과격한 스포츠가 재미있고 안전할 수도 있다는 것을 보여주었다. 암벽 등반은 그런 스포츠들 중 하나이다. 암벽 등반이 점점 인기를 얻는 데는 몇 가지 이유가 있

다. 암벽 등반은 점점 안전해지고 있다. 회사들이 꾸준히 안전한 암벽 등반 장치들을 만든다. 오래 전에는 암벽 등반 안전 장치의 질이 좋지 않아서 사용하기에 그렇게 안전하지 못했다. 요즘의 안전 장비들은 코끼리를 들어도 고장 나지 않을 만큼 강하다.

더 좋은 건축 자재로 실제처럼 보이는 실내 암벽을 만들 수 있게 되었다. 이로 인해 많은 초보자들이 최소의 위험으로 적절한 지도를 받아 안전하게 연습을 할 수 있다. 그들은 정확한 등반 방법을 배우고 실제 산에서의 암벽 등반에 대비한다.

오래되고 잘못된 정보들 때문에 많은 사람들은 암벽 등반이 위험하다고 생각했었다. 인터넷은 사람들이 암벽 등반에 대해 더 잘 이해하도록 도왔다. 따라서 더 많은 사람들이 암벽 등반에 관심을 갖게 되었다.

iBT Practice 2   p.42

1. (B)   2. (D)
3. Yes: (A), (C) / No: (B), (D)

Listen to part of a conversation between two friends.

W: So many people watch the Olympics. I think it is the most popular program on TV.
M: No, it's not. The World Cup is the most popular event.
W: Are you sure? There are more than 100 countries that take part in the Olympics.
M: That is true. Still, more people watch the World Cup.
W: Wow, I didn't know that. How many people watch the World Cup?
M: It's different every time. In 2002, there were 25 days of games. In that time, an average of over 1 billion people watched the World Cup per day. FIFA said that the 2002 World Cup was the most successful World Cup so far.
W: That is a lot. Which country do you think watched the most?
M: n my opinion, China has the highest population, so they probably watched the most. During the World Cup, I think almost everyone in the world watched the games. Most South Koreans watched the World Cup.
W: Oh, I heard that South Korea made a record for cheering outside in the streets. Over 4 million people watched the game between Korea and Italy in the streets. You know what? I was one of them!

W: 정말 많은 사람들이 올림픽 경기를 봐. 내 생각엔 올림픽 중계가 TV에서 가장 인기 있는 프로그램 같아.
M: 아냐 그렇지 않아. 월드컵이 제일 인기 있는 경기야.
W: 진짜야? 올림픽은 참가국만 100개국이 넘는데.
M: 그건 그렇지. 하지만 더 많은 사람들이 월드컵을 봐.
W: 와, 그건 몰랐네. 얼마나 많은 사람들이 월드컵을 보는데?
M: 그때그때마다 다른데 2002년에는 25일 동안 경기를 했어. 그 당시 하루에 평균 10억 이상의 사람들이 월드컵을 봤어. FIFA에서는 2002 월드컵이 지금까지의 월드컵 중 가장 성공적이었다고 발표를 했어.
W: 정말 많구나. 어느 나라에서 제일 많이 시청했다고 생각해?
M: 내 생각엔 중국이 인구가 제일 많으니까 가장 많이 봤겠지. 월드컵 기간 동안 전세계 모든 사람들이 게임을 봤을 것 같아. 한국 사람 대부분이 월드컵을 봤으니까.
W: 아, 한국이 길거리 응원으로 기록을 세웠다고 들었어. 4백만 명도 넘는 사람들이 한국과 이탈리아의 경기를 거리에서 봤어. 그거 알아? 나도 그 중 하나였어!

Word Review   p.46

1. immediately   2. protective
3. minimum   4. court
5. sweep   6. jail
7. equipment   8. religion
9. take part in 10. due to
11. An average of 12. refuses to

Chapter 3
Animals
/ Organization

Overview p.51
Sample Question: (D)

Basic Drills 1 p.52
1. (C)   2. (A)

1. Kangaroos have a <u>different</u> <u>way</u> of raising babies. The mother <u>gives</u> <u>birth</u> to a 2.5 cm baby. The baby stays in the mother's pouch and drinks milk. When the baby is <u>three</u> <u>months</u> <u>old</u>, it starts to play outside of the mother's pouch. When the baby is ten months old, the baby <u>leaves</u> <u>the</u> <u>pouch</u> completely.

   캥거루는 다른 방식으로 새끼를 기른다. 어미 캥거루는 2.5 센티미터 크기의 새끼를 낳는다. 새끼는 어미의 육아낭에서 머물면서 젖을 먹는다. 새끼가 3개월째 되면 어미의 육아낭 밖에서 놀기 시작한다. 10개월이 되면 새끼는 완전히 육아낭을 떠난다.

2. M: What is the largest animal <u>that</u> <u>ever</u> <u>lived</u> on earth?
   W: That's easy. It's the blue whale.
   M: Are you serious? I thought <u>it</u> <u>would</u> <u>have</u> <u>been</u> a dinosaur.
   W: No, the blue whale is <u>larger</u> <u>than</u> any dinosaur.
   M: How about the smallest?
   W: <u>The</u> <u>smallest</u> <u>animal</u> would have to be an amoeba.

   M: 지구상에 살았던 동물 중에 가장 큰 동물은 뭘까?
   W: 그거야 쉽지. 흰긴수염고래잖아.
   M: 진짜야? 난 공룡인 줄 알았는데.
   W: 아냐, 흰긴수염고래는 어떤 공룡보다도 커.
   M: 그럼 가장 작은 동물은?
   W: 가장 작은 동물은 아메바가 되겠지.

Basic Drills 2 p.53
On Your Own

Possible Answer
1. (1) junior   (2) question
   (3) example   (4) second
2. (1) A.   (2) benft
   (3) no. / No.   (4) newsppr
3. (1) Mozt. grt compsr = 18C.
   (2) In 1950s Afrcn-Amrcns mistrt Amrcn socty

3. (1) Mozart was a great composer during the 18th century.
   (2) In the 1950s, African-Americans were mistreated in American society.

Listenining Practice ❶ p.54
1. (C)   2. (B)

There are many animals on earth. Some animals are very big, and some are very small. Humans are animals too, but we are physically different from other animals in certain ways.

We are the only animals in the world that walk on two legs. No other animal can walk on two legs for a long time. Animals need to walk on four legs for speed, and to jump. The design of the bones in humans is different from other animals. Because of this, only humans sleep looking up, and all other animals sleep looking down.

In addition, humans are one of the few animals in the world without a tail. Scientists think that humans once had a tail, but lost it as we did not need one. However, most other animals, such as the cheetahs, need their tails. Their tails are used to balance themselves when they run.

지구상에는 많은 동물들이 있다. 어떤 동물들은 아주 크고 어떤 동물들은 매우 작다. 인간도 역시 동물이지만 우리는 어떤 면에서는 다른 동물들과 육체적으로 다르다.

우리는 두 다리로 걸을 수 있는 지상의 유일한 동물이다. 오랫동안 두 발로 걸을 수 있는 동물은 없다. 동물은 속도를 내거나 점프를 하려면 네 발을 모두 써야 한다. 인간의 뼈의 구조는 다른 동물들과는 다르다. 이로 인해 인간만이 (누워서) 위를 보고 자고 다른 동물들은 (엎드려서) 아래를 보고 잔다.

그뿐 아니라, 인간은 꼬리가 없는 몇 안되는 동물 중 하나이다. 과학자들은 인간은 원래 꼬리가 있었지만 필요가 없어지자 사라졌다고 한다. 그러나 치타와 같은 동물들은 꼬리가 필요하다. 치타의 꼬리는 달릴 때 균형을 잡는 기능을 한다.

Listenining Practice ❷ p.55

1. (C)   2. (B)

M: Hi, Sylvia. Where are you going?
W: I've got a lot of things to do today. I am taking my dog to the vet in the afternoon.
M: Why? Is there anything wrong with your dog?
W: No, he is very healthy. I always get him a checkup even if he is healthy.
M: How often do you take him for a checkup?
W: I take him to the vet every six months. Just to be sure, I also feed him some medicine. If I don't give my dog that medicine, he can become very sick.
M: Oh, that would be terrible. It sounds like a lot of work is needed to keep dogs healthy. Is there anything else?
W: I also take him out for walks every day. That way, both he and I get some exercise. That's how owners take care of their dogs properly.

M: 안녕 실비아. 어디 가니?
W: 오늘 할 일이 많아. 오후에는 강아지 데리고 동물 병원에 갈 거야.
M: 왜? 강아지가 어디 아파?
W: 아니 아주 건강해. 건강해도 검진을 받게 하는 거야.
M: 얼마나 자주 검진 받으러 가는데?
W: 6개월마다 한번씩 수의사한테 가. 좀 더 신경쓰느라 약도 먹이고 있어. 그 약을 먹이지 않으면 병이 날수도 있어서.
M: 아 그럼 안되지. 강아지를 건강하게 기르려면 할 일이 많은 것 같다. 또 다른 건 없어?
W: 매일 데리고 나와서 산책을 시켜주지. 그럼 나도 개도 운동을 할 수가 있어. 그것이 개들을 건강하게 기르는 방법이지.

Listenining Practice ❸ p.56

1. Yes: (B), (D) / No: (A), (C)   2. (D)

There are many large animals in the world. Elephants are large, but they are small when compared to the largest animal in the world, the blue whale.

Baby blue whales are big, even when they are only babies. At birth, they are about 7 meters long and weigh 2 tons. They drink 200 liters of milk every day, and they grow about 80 kg every day. In fact, they grow so quickly that we can hear them grow.

The young whales stay with their mothers until they are a year old. During that time, the young whale learns to live in the ocean. The mother whale teaches the young whale to hunt and fight off enemies.

When young whales become adults, they are about 30 meters long and weigh about 130 tons. Adult blue whales can eat over 4000 kg of food every day.

세상에는 많은 대형 동물들이 있다. 코끼리는 크지만 지상에서 가장 큰 동물인 흰긴수염고래에 비하면 작다.

새끼 고래일지라도 아기 흰긴수염고래는 엄청 크다. 태어날 때 몸길이는 약 7미터 정도이고 몸무게는 2톤 가량 나간다. 그들은 매일 200리터의 젖을 먹고 하루에 80킬로그램씩 성장한다. 사실 성장 속도가 너무 빨라서 자라는 소리가 들릴 정도이다.

어린 고래들은 한살이 될 때까지 어미 옆에 있는다. 그 기간 동안에 아기 고래는 바다에서 사는 법을 배운다. 어미는 어린 고래에게 먹이 잡는 법과 적들과 싸우는 법을 가르친다.

어린 고래가 다 자라면 몸 길이는 30미터 정도 되고 130톤이 나간다. 다 자란 흰긴수염고래는 매일 4,000킬로그램 이상의 먹이를 먹는다.

Listenining Practice ❹ p.57

1. (D)   2. (A)

M: Have you heard of Dian Fossey?

W: Who is that? I've not heard of her.
M: She was the famous scientist who spent a lot of time studying gorillas. In fact, she was the first human to touch a gorilla and work with them.
W: Oh, I remember her. I heard that even movies were made about her.
M: Yes, that's her. She started the 'Dian Fossey Gorilla Fund International' to help gorillas in Africa. Many hunters were killing gorillas in the mountains. There were less than 650 gorillas in the world when she started the organization.
W: Wow. She is an amazing woman. Is she still working to save the gorillas?
M: Unfortunately, Dian was murdered in her home in Africa. Nobody knows who killed her, but some people think that it was a hunter who did not like her work.
W: Oh, that is such tragic news.
M: 다이안 퍼씨에 대해 들어봤니?
W: 그게 누군데? 처음 들어봐.
M: 많은 시간을 고릴라 연구에 바친 유명한 과학자야. 사실 고릴라와 접촉하고 함께 생활했던 최초의 인간이야.
W: 아 생각난다. 그 여자에 관한 영화도 만들어졌다고 들었어.
M: 그래 맞아. 아프리카의 고릴라를 살리기 위해 '다이안 퍼씨 국제 고릴라 기금'을 설립했어. 많은 사냥꾼들이 산에 살고 있는 고릴라들을 죽였었어. 처음 그 기구를 만들었을 때는 전 세계에 고릴라가 650마리도 안됐었어.
W: 와 정말 대단한 여자구나. 아직도 고릴라 구하는 일을 하고 있니?
M: 불행하게도 다이안은 아프리카에 있는 자신의 집에서 살해됐어. 아무도 누가 그녀를 죽였는지 모르지만 몇몇 사람들은 그녀의 일을 못마땅하던 사냥꾼의 짓이라고 생각해.
W: 아, 정말 비극적인 얘기다.

Listenining Practice ⑤   p.58

| 1. (A)   2. (B) |

There are many slow animals in the world. You might have heard of snails and turtles being slow animals, but how many people have heard of the laziest animal in the world? Scientists think the three-toed sloth is the laziest animal in the world. The three-toed sloth hangs on trees, and it is common for the sloth to spend their whole life in just one tree. They only come down the tree about every 8 days because they do not like to move. They move at a speed of 1.5 meters a minute.

The three-toed sloth sleeps for nearly 20 hours a day, and moves only to eat. Since it hardly moves, many insects live in the fur of the sloth. The larger insects eat smaller insects living in the fur of the sloth. The sloth always moves very slowly unless it is attacked by an enemy.

세상에는 느린 동물들이 많이 있다. 달팽이나 거북이가 느리다는 것은 들어봤을 테지만 얼마나 많은 사람들이 세상에서 가장 게으른 동물에 대해 알고 있을까? 학자들은 세발가락 나무늘보가 세상에서 가장 게으른 동물이라고 한다.

세발가락나무늘보는 나무에 매달려있다. 나무늘보는 평생 하나의 나무에서만 생활하는 것이 일반적인 일이다. 그들은 움직이기를 싫어해서 대략 8일에 한번 정도 나무에서 내려온다. 1분에 1.5미터 정도의 속도로 움직인다.

세발가락나무늘보는 하루에 20시간 가량을 자고 오로지 먹을 때만 움직인다. 거의 움직이지 않기 때문에 나무늘보의 털 속에는 많은 곤충들이 살고 있다. 나무늘보의 털 속에 사는 큰 곤충들은 털 속의 더 작은 곤충들을 먹고 산다. 이 동물들은 적으로부터 공격을 당하지 않으면 항상 그렇듯이 느리게 움직인다.

Listenining Practice ⑥   p.59

| 1. (B)   2. (A) |

T: Does anyone keep pets at home?
M: I keep fish in my room.
W: I had a dog, but it died.
T: Oh, I'm sorry to hear that. Anyway, doctors say that pets are healthy for people.
M: How can pets make people healthy? Some people are allergic to fur, and pets can also carry diseases.
T: Well, besides that problem, pets can help owners become healthy. Most pets need exercise. Owners have to exercise with them.
W: I agree. I used to take my dogs out for a walk every day.
M: Well, since fish do not need exercise, I don't

think they will help me.

T: No, you're wrong. Just by looking at them, you reduce stress. Science has proven that people who have pets live longer, and are happier.

M: I guess that is true. Fish might not fetch a ball or bark, but I feel better when I see them.

T: 집에서 애완동물을 기르는 사람?
M: 저는 방에서 물고기를 길러요.
W: 저는 개 한 마리가 있었는데 죽었어요.
T: 저런 안됐구나. 어쨌든 의사들 말로는 애완동물이 사람의 건강에 좋대.
M: 어떻게 애완동물이 사람을 건강하게 하죠? 어떤 사람들은 털에 알레르기가 있고 병을 옮기는 동물들도 있는데.
T: 글쎄, 그런 문제들이 있음에도 불구하고, 애완동물들은 주인들이 건강해지도록 돕는단다. 대부분의 동물들은 운동이 필요해. 주인들은 그 동물들과 함께 운동을 해야 하지.
W: 그건 동감이에요. 저도 매일 개 산책을 시키러 나갔었어요.
M: 음, 물고기는 운동이 필요 없으니까 내 건강에는 별로 도움이 안되겠네요.
T: 아냐, 그렇지 않아. 그냥 바라보는 것 만으로도 스트레스가 줄어들어. 과학적으로 애완동물을 키우는 사람들이 더 오래 살고 행복하다는 것이 입증 되었어.
M: 맞는 것 같아요. 물고기가 공을 물어오거나 짖지는 않지만 보고 있으면 기분이 좋아져요.

iBT Practice 1   p.60

1. (A)   2. (C)   3. (D)

Listen to part of a talk in a biology class.

Most animals have no problem seeing, because they are active during the day. However, night animals are a little bit different. They are animals that become active at night. These animals use other senses, such as hearing, taste or touch to hunt at night.

For example, bats have eyes, but they do not use them. Instead, they see by using their ears. They make sounds and listen to the echoes bounce off objects. This tells them what is close to them, and what is farther away. It is a very effective way of seeing things. In fact, it is so effective that blind people have used this method to "see" successfully.

Owls use both sight and sound to hunt for food. They have very big eyes, and they can only see straight ahead. Owls must turn their heads to see left and right. This is because the owls' sensitive ears are on their face. Since their eyes do not move, they find the location of mice easily by simply looking at where the sound is coming from. The owl can also hear sounds from very far away.

대부분의 동물들은 낮에 주로 활동하기 때문에 앞을 보는데 아무런 문제가 없다. 그러나 야행성 동물들은 조금 다르다. 그들은 밤에 더 활발해진다. 이런 동물들은 청각, 미각 또는 촉각 같은 다른 감각을 이용해 밤에 먹이를 잡는다.

예를 들어, 박쥐는 눈이 있지만 사용하지는 않는다. 그 대신 귀를 통해 사물을 확인한다. 그들은 소리를 내서 물체에서 반사되는 메아리를 듣는다. 그러면 어떤 것이 가까이 있고 어떤 것이 멀리 떨어져 있는지 알게 된다. 이것은 사물을 확인하는데 아주 효과적인 방법이다. 사실 이 방법은 아주 효율적이어서 어떤 맹인들은 이런 메아리를 듣는 방법을 사용해서 사물을 정확하게 확인한다.

올빼미는 시력과 청력을 이용해 먹이를 사냥한다. 올빼미는 아주 큰 눈을 가지고 있는데 오로지 정면 방향으로만 볼 수 있다. 올빼미는 왼쪽이나 오른쪽을 보기 위해서는 고개를 돌려야 한다. 그 이유는 올빼미의 민감한 귀가 얼굴에 있기 때문이다. 그들의 눈은 움직이지 않아서 소리가 들리는 방향을 봄으로써 먹이의 위치를 알아낼 수 있다. 올빼미는 아주 먼 곳의 소리도 들을 수 있다.

iBT Practice 2   p.62

1. (C)   2. (A)
3. Yes: (B), (D) / No: (A), (C)

Listen to a conversation between two friends.

W: There are so many animal names to learn!
M: If you think there are a lot, you should also know that there are separate names for male, female and baby animals too.
W: What do you mean?
M: I'm sure you have heard of a male chicken being called a rooster and a female chicken a hen.
W: Yes, that much I know, but do all animals have

different names for males and females?
M: Most animals do have them. Some animals share the same names too. Males of large animals are called bulls, and females are called cows. Their baby is called a calf.
W: Aren't they the names of cows?
M: Yes, you are right. But even if the animal is not a cow, such as a crocodile or a whale, they are still called bulls and cows.
W: That is incredible. I didn't know any of that.
M: Also, male cats are tomcats, females are queens, and babies are kittens. I'll tell you one more. Male kangaroos are called jacks, and female kangaroos are called jills. Baby kangaroos are called joeys.
W: Wow, there seems to be so much that I still need to learn.

W: 알아야 할 동물 이름들이 너무 많아.
M: 그렇게 생각한다면 암컷, 수컷, 새끼들을 부르는 이름들이 다 따로 있다는 것도 알아야겠구나.
W: 무슨 소리야?
M: 수탉은 rooster라고 하고 암탉은 hen이라고 하는 건 알고 있겠지.
W: 그래, 그 정도야 알지만, 모든 동물들이 암컷과 수컷마다 다른 이름이 있다는 거야?
M: 대부분의 동물들은 그래. 어떤 동물들은 똑같은 이름으로 불리기도 해. 큰 동물들의 수컷은 bull이라고 하고 암컷은 cow라고 해. 새끼는 calf고.
W: 그건 소이름들 아니야?
M: 맞아. 그런데 소가 아니라고 할지라도 악어나 고래 처럼 큰 동물들도 그렇게 부르지.
W: 놀라운걸. 난 전혀몰랐어.
M: 뿐만아니라, 숫고양이는 tomcat, 암컷은 queen 그리고 새끼는 kitten이야. 하나만 더 알려주지. 수컷 캥거루는 jack, 암컷 캥거루는 jill, 아기 캥거루는 joey라고 불러.
W: 와, 배워야 할 게 아직도 많이 있는것 같구나.

Word Review p.66

1. tragic	2. object
3. temperature	4. vet
5. pouch	6. sweat
7. insect	8. echo
9. straight ahead	10. bounce off
11. take care of	12. gave birth to

Chapter 4

Plants
/ Organization-Rhetorical Connection

Overview   p.71

Sample Question: (C)

Basic Drills 1   p.72

1. (C)   2. (A)

1. Humans cannot live on this earth <u>without eating plants</u>. Doctors say that we must eat a lot of vegetables to have <u>a balanced diet</u> because they contain minerals and fiber. Fruits are also plants. We get most of our vitamins and sugar <u>from fruits</u>. Fruits, such as oranges, have <u>plenty of</u> vitamin C.

   인간은 식물을 먹지 않고는 지구상에서 살 수가 없다. 의사들은 우리가 균형 있는 식생활을 하기 위해 많은 야채를 먹어야 한다고 말한다. 야채 안에는 무기질과 섬유질이 있기 때문이다. 과일도 역시 식물이다. 우리는 과일에서 비타민과 당분을 섭취한다. 오렌지와 같은 과일에는 비타민 C가 풍부하다.

2. There are <u>many types</u> of fruits in this world. However, no country can grow all the fruits of the world <u>at once</u>. The weather is very important to grow fruits. For instance, <u>in hot climates</u>, there are a lot of mangoes and melons. <u>In colder climates</u>, there are many strawberries and apples.

   세상에는 많은 종류의 과일이 있다, 그렇지만 한번에 전세계 모든 과일을 재배할 수 있는 나라는 없다. 날씨가 과일을 재배하는데 아주 중요하다. 예를 들어, 더운 기후에서는 망고와 멜론이 잘 자란다. 서늘한 기후에서는 딸기와 사과가 잘 자란다.

Basic Drills 2   p.73

On Your Own

Possible Answer

1. (1) department   (2) important
   (3) language   (4) information
2. (1) probs   (2) transptn
   (3) elvtr   (4) max
3. (1) We shld. b. hrng. ← Dept. Transptn.
   (2) U shld. travl. resrvtn. → forgn. cntry.

3. (1) We should be hearing back from the Department of Transportation.
   (2) You should make travel reservations when you go to a foreign country.

Listenining Practice ❶   p.74

1. (B)   2. (A)

When we get sick, we take medicine. Different things are mixed to make medicine that can fight off sickness and make us feel better. One of those things in medicine is plants.

Plants are a very important part of traditional medicine. Plants used in traditional medicine are called herbs. Many different types of herbs are used in medicine. Some herbs can be expensive, or they can be very cheap.

Plants also play a very important part in modern medicine. More and more plants are used in making modern medicine. Medicine companies are always trying to use herbs in their medicine. In fact, scientists are now trying to study more about plants under the sea as only 5% of sea plants have been tested so far.

우리는 몸이 아프면 약을 먹는다. 병과 싸우고 몸을 낫게 할 수 있는 약을 만들기 위해서는 여러 다른 재료들이 섞이게 된다. 약에 사용하는 그런 물질들 중 하나가 식물이다.

식물은 전통 의학에서 아주 중요한 부분을 차지한다. 전통 의학에서 사용하는 식물은 허브라고 불린다. 많은 종류의 허브들이 약품에 사용된다. 어떤 허브들은 비싸고, 또 어떤 것들은 아주 싸다.

식물은 현대 의학에서도 중요한 부분을 차지한다. 점점 더 많은 식물들이 현대 의약품에 사용된다. 제약회사는 언제나 자신들의 약품에 허브의 사용을 시도한다. 실제로 과학자들은 바다 식물들을 제약에 이용하려는 시도를 하고 있다. 지금까지는 바다 식물의 5%만이 실험되었다.

Listenining Practice ❷ p.75

1. (C)   2. (B)

W: Did you know that there are billions of animals and plants that live in the sea?
M: I know fish live in the sea, but plants? I have not heard of such a thing.
W: Seaweed is a sea plant, but that's only one type. In fact, most of the world's oxygen comes from sea plants.
M: What? Now you're really joking. Everyone knows that trees give us oxygen.
W: Yes, plants on land give out oxygen too. There are a lot of very small plants floating in the sea that produce oxygen. These plants in the sea produce a thousand times more oxygen than all the trees in the world.
M: Wow, I didn't know that. We should take care of our oceans better. I don't want the ocean to stop producing oxygen.
W: Yes, that is an important reason to keep the sea clean.

W: 바닷속에 수십억 종류의 동식물이 살고 있다는 거 알았니?
M: 물고기가 바다에 사는 건 알겠는데 식물이라고? 그런 얘기는 들어본 적이 없는데.
W: 해초가 바닷속 식물 중 하나야 하지만 그건 한 종류에 불과하지. 사실 세계 산소의 대부분이 해조류에서 나와.
M: 뭐? 농담하는 거야? 나무가 우리가 숨 쉴 수 있는 산소를 준다는 건 모두 알고 있지.
W: 그래, 육상 식물도 산소를 방출하지. 바다 속을 떠다니면서 산소를 생산하는 아주 작은 식물들도 있어. 바닷속의 이런 식물들이 전 세계에 있는 나무 전체보다 천 배 이상의 산소를 만들어내.
M: 와, 그건 몰랐어. 우리가 바다를 더 잘 돌봐야겠어. 바다가 산소 생산을 멈추게 하면 안 되지.
W: 그래, 그게 바로 바다를 깨끗이 지켜야 하는 중요한 이유지.

Listenining Practice ❸ p.76

1. (C)   2. (A)

M: I have to write a report about the food chain for next week's class.
W: Oh, that's a really interesting topic. It describes the cycle of animals and plants.
M: What do you mean?
W: irst, small animals eat plants, such as fruits and nuts. Then, larger animals, such as eagles or snakes, catch smaller animals for food. Finally, when these larger animals die, the ground absorbs their bodies, and the plants use them for food.
M: Wow! Are you sure about that?
W: Yes, that is the food chain. Some people call this process a life cycle.
M: Could you tell me more about this food chain process? It sounds really interesting. I can't believe I didn't know about this until you told me.
W: Sure, I could tell you more about it later. Meet me after lunch in the playground.

M: 다음주 수업을 위해 먹이사슬에 관한 보고서를 써야 해.
W: 아 그거 정말 재미있는 주제다. 동물과 식물의 순환을 설명하는 거지.
M: 무슨 뜻이니?
W: 먼저 작은 동물이 과일이나 견과류 같은 식물을 먹지. 그 다음 독수리나 뱀 같은 큰 동물들은 작은 동물들을 먹이로 삼아. 마지막으로 이 큰 동물들이 죽으면 토양은 그들의 몸을 흡수해서 식물들이 그것을 먹이로 쓴다는 거지.
M: 와! 그게 사실이야?
W: 그래 그게 먹이사슬이야. 어떤 사람들은 이런 과정을 생태순환이라고도 부르고.
M: 먹이사슬 과정에 대해 더 얘기해 줄 수 있겠니? 정말 재미있다. 네가 말 해줄 때까지 모르고 있었다니.
W: 물론이지, 더 얘기해 줄 수 있어. 점심 먹고 운동장에서 보자.

Listenining Practice ❹ p.77

1. (A)   2. (C)

All living things on earth grow at different

speeds. Some quick growing plants, like bamboo, are widely used for many reasons.

Bamboo is very cheap, because it is the fastest growing plant in the world. Baby bamboo grows at about 1 meter in 24 hours for the first few days, and grows slower to about 20 meters in 60 days. In contrast, trees may take 60 years to grow 20 meters. Bamboo is also cheap because it grows in large groups, and one group can produce many meters of bamboo in a short period of time.

Bamboo is also the strongest plant in the world. This is why bamboo is used in so many different parts of the world. Bamboo is used for the main structure of many homes in Bangladesh and Burma. Bamboo is also used by workers in China and Hong Kong instead of steel safety bars when making tall buildings.

지구상의 살아있는 모든 생물들은 서로 다른 속도로 성장을 한다. 대나무처럼 빨리 자라는 식물들은 여러 가지 이유에서 널리 이용된다.

대나무는 값이 싸다. 왜냐하면 세상에서 가장 빨리 자라는 식물이기 때문이다. 어린 대나무는 처음 몇 일 동안 24시간에 약 1미터씩 자라고, 60일간은 20미터 정도의 길이까지 천천히 자란다. 이에 반해 일반 나무들은 20미터가 자라는데 60년 정도가 걸린다. 대나무는 큰 군락을 이루어 자라는데, 한 군락에서 짧은 기간 내에 많은 양의 나무를 생산할 수 있기 때문에 가격이 싸다.

대나무는 세상에서 가장 강한 식물이다. 그렇기 때문에 전 세계 많은 지역에서 사용된다. 대나무는 방글라데시나 버마에서 많은 집의 주요 골조로 사용된다. 중국이나 홍콩의 일꾼들은 높은 건물을 짓는데 쓰는 쇠로 된 안전막대 대신 대나무를 사용하기도 한다.

Listenining Practice ⑤   p.78

1. (B)   2. (A)

W: Did you know that not all paper is made from wood?
M: Isn't all paper made from wood?
W: No. As a matter of fact, paper made from wood is only one type of paper. There is paper that does not use wood.
M: You're kidding! How else do they make paper? I thought we need big factories to make paper from wood.
W: Not really. Long ago, people used different types of paper. The Egyptians used papyrus, made from other plants. The Chinese used paper that used old rags.
M: Rags? Are you sure about that?
W: Yes. Rags were made from plants, so rag paper wasn't very different from paper made from wood.
M: Hmm ... Do you think you can tell me more about it after class? I'd love to hear more about it.
W: Sure, it's not a problem.

W: 나무로만 종이를 만들 수 있는 건 아니라는 거 알고 있었니?
M: 종이는 다 나무로 만드는 거 아냐?
W: 아냐. 사실 나무로 만드는 종이는 종이의 한 종류에 불과해. 나무를 쓰지 않고 만드는 종이도 있어.
M: 농담이지! 그럼 어떻게 종이를 만들어? 나무로 종이를 만들려면 큰 공장이 필요할 거라고 생각했었는데.
W: 그렇지 않아. 오래 전에 사람들은 다른 종류의 종이를 사용했어. 이집트인들은 나무와는 다른 식물로 만든 파피루스를 사용했어. 중국인들은 오래된 헝겊 조각 같은 걸로 종이를 만들었어.
M: 헝겊 조각이라구? 정말?
W: 그래. 헝겊 역시 식물에서 나오는 거야, 그래서 헝겊으로 만든 종이도 나무로 만든 종이와 별로 다르지는 않아.
M: 음… 이따 수업 끝나고 더 얘기해 줄 수 있니? 정말 더 듣고 싶어.
W: 그래, 좋아.

Listenining Practice ⑥   p.79

1. (D)   2. (B)

Everyone knows that plants and animals are very different. The biggest difference is that plants do not have a mouth to eat and a brain to think like animals. Plants also have very different cells from animals.

Most plants use a process called "photosynthesis" to get energy from the sun, not like animals, which have to eat to get energy. The leaves of the plant change light into energy that the plant can use. When plants change light to energy, they release oxygen into the air.

Plants also have a different cell structure from animal cells. Plants have something called a cell wall. These walls are why plants break and not bend like animal skin. This is needed because plants do not have muscles to shape themselves.

사람들은 식물과 동물이 아주 다르다는 것을 알고 있다. 가장 큰 차이는 식물은 동물처럼 먹을 수 있는 입과 생각할 수 있는 뇌가 없는 것이다. 그리고 식물은 동물과 아주 다른 세포를 가지고 있다.

대부분의 식물은 에너지를 얻기 위해 먹어야 하는 동물과 달리 광합성이라는 과정을 통해 태양으로부터 에너지를 얻는다. 식물의 잎은 빛을 식물이 사용할 수 있는 에너지로 바꾼다. 식물은 빛을 에너지로 바꾸면서 공기 중에 산소를 방출한다.

식물은 동물의 세포와 다른 구조의 세포를 갖고 있다. 식물은 세포벽이라는 것을 가지고 있다. 이 벽 때문에 식물이 동물의 피부처럼 구부러지지 않고 부러지는 것이다. 식물에는 자신의 모양을 잡을 근육이 없기 때문에 세포벽이 필요하다.

that melts insects for food. Ants and other small insects think that there is a lot of food inside the pitcher. The insect will try to see what is inside the pitcher. The sides of the pitcher walls are very slippery, and the insect falls to the bottom of the pitcher.

육식 동물은 사자나 호랑이처럼 일생 동안 고기만을 먹는 동물이다. 세상의 많은 동물들이 육식동물이다. 신기하게도 식물들 중에도 육식을 해서 식충식물이라고 불리는 것들이 있다.

끈끈이주걱은 유명한 식충식물이다. 끈끈이주걱은 파리를 잡을 수 있는 커다란 덫이 있다. 파리는 덫의 냄새를 맡고 그게 먹이라고 생각을 한다. 파리가 그 근처에 앉으면 다리가 식물에 붙어버린다. 식물은 덫을 닫고 천천히 녹여서 파리를 먹는다.

또 다른 식충식물은 벌레잡이통풀이다. 이 식물의 꽃은 우스꽝스러운 물통처럼 생겼다. 그것은 식물의 잎의 끝부분에 달려있다. 벌레잡이통풀도 냄새로 곤충을 유인한다. 그 식물의 바닥에는 강력한 액체가 있어서 곤충을 녹여 먹이로 쓴다. 개미와 다른 작은 곤충들은 그 통풀안에 많은 먹이가 들어있을 것이라고 생각한다. 곤충은 통풀안에 뭐가 있는지 보려고 한다. 그러다 통풀의 벽면이 아주 미끄러워서 곤충은 통풀안으로 떨어지고 만다.

iBT Practice 1   p.80

1. (B)   2. (D)
3. Yes: (A), (D) / No: (B), (C)

Listen to part of a talk in a science class.

Carnivores are animals that only eat meat their whole lives, such as lions and tigers. Many animals in the world are carnivores. Strangely, there are some plants that are also carnivores because they eat meat.

The Venus flytrap is a well-known carnivore. The Venus flytrap has a large trap to catch flies. The flies smell the trap and think that it is food. When the fly lands on the area, the legs get stuck on the plant. The plant closes the trap and slowly eats the fly by melting it.

Another carnivorous plant is the pitcher plant. The flower of the plant looks like a funny water bottle. It hangs on the end of the plant leaves. The pitcher plant also attracts insects by smell. The bottom of the pitcher contains a powerful liquid

iBT Practice 2   p.82

1. (C)   2. (C)   3. (B), (C)

Listen to part of a conversation between two friends.

M: My teacher told us to find out about the most expensive food in the world. Could you tell me what it is?

W: Well, some people say that the truffle is the most expensive. It is a mushroom, and there are many types of truffles. The most expensive truffles grow only in Europe.

M: Mushrooms? Are you joking?

W: No, I'm not. Truffles grow on roots of pine trees. Naturally, truffles grow underground. That is why it is very hard for people to find them.

M: Then how do the farmers find these mushrooms?

W: Trained pigs or dogs find truffles by smell. They are the only animals that people use to find truffles. Truffles are also expensive because

they take a very long time to grow.
M: Well, how expensive are the buried mushrooms? After all, it's only a mushroom.
W: The highest truffle prices that I have heard of are nearly 2,000,000 won for 1 kilogram.
M: What! That's so expensive! Just how do people eat truffles?
W: People cut them into very thin slices and serve them together with steak or other types of food as topping. I'll tell you about the taste of truffles when we get the chance. I'm going home now.
M: 선생님께서 세상에서 가장 비싼 음식을 알아오라고 하셨어. 너는 그게 뭔지 아니?
W: 글쎄, 사람들 말로는 트러플이 가장 비싼 음식이라고 하던데. 그건 버섯종류인데 트러플에도 여러 종류가 있어. 가장 비싼 트러플은 유럽에서만 자라지.
M: 버섯? 농담하니?
W: 아냐 진짜야. 트러플은 소나무 뿌리에서 자라. 원래 트러플은 땅 속에 있어. 그렇기 때문에 사람들이 찾기가 어려운 거야.
M: 그러면 농부들은 어떻게 이 버섯을 찾아내지?
W: 훈련된 돼지나 개가 냄새로 트러플을 찾아내. 걔네들은 트러플을 찾을 수 있는 유일한 동물들이야. 또 트러플은 자라는데 아주 긴 시간이 걸리기 때문에 비싸.
M: 그럼 그 땅에 묻힌 버섯이 얼마나 비싼데? 비싸 봤자 버섯일 텐데.
W: 내가 듣기론 최상의 트러플은 1킬로그램에 200만원가까이 한다고 했어.
M: 와! 정말 비싸네! 트러플은 어떻게 요리해서 먹어?
W: 버섯을 아주 얇게 썰어서 스테이크나 다른 종류의 음식과 함께 토핑으로 쓰는 거야. 다음에 기회가 되면 트러플 맛에 대해 얘기 해줄께. 나 지금 집에 가는 중이야.

Word Review p.86

1. cell
2. climate
3. melt
4. absorb
5. trap
6. float
7. attract
8. oxygen
9. plenty of
10. instead of
11. at once
12. are made of

Chapter 5

Travel
/ Content-Identifying Relationship

Overview p.91

Sample Question: (B)

Basic Drills 1 p.92

1. (A)   2. (B)

1. Buildings and towers always stand straight. However, there is one very famous tower that leans. The Leaning Tower of Pisa in Italy currently leans at an angle. The tower started leaning because it was built on soft ground. Even though the tower is leaning, many people take pictures of the tower.
건물과 탑은 언제나 똑바로 서있다. 하지만 기울어진 유명한 탑이 하나 있다. 이탈리아의 피사의 사탑은 현재 비스듬히 서있다. 피사의 사탑은 부드러운 지반에 세워져서 기울어지기 시작했다. 탑이 비록 기울어져 있어도 많은 사람들은 그 탑의 사진을 찍는다.

2. Among the ancient wonders of the world are the pyramids in Egypt. The pyramids are graves for Egyptian kings and queens. The pyramids are very big, even bigger than a football field. The entrances to the pyramids are very complicated, as the designers did not want people to steal the Pharaoh's gold.
세계의 고대 기적 중 하나는 이집트의 피라미드다. 피라미드는 이집트 왕과 여왕의 무덤이다. 이것은 축구장보다도 훨씬 크다. 피라미드의 입구는 설계자가 파라오의 황금을 훔쳐가지 못하도록 만들었기 때문에 굉장히 복잡하다.

Basic Drills 2 p.93

On Your Own

Possible Answer

1. (1) Earth is the third planet from the sun.
   (2) He knew how to fly the plane.
   (3) Cars and buses cause pollution to the environment.
2. (1) NY ≠ captl US
   (2) Dr. advs U ≠ mix medcn w/ alchl
   (3) Choclt most poplr sweet

2. (1) New York is not the capital city of the United States.
   (2) Doctors advise that you never mix medicine with alcohol.
   (3) Chocolate is probably the most popular sweet in the world.

Listenining Practice ❶ p.94

1. (D)   2. (B)

Weather can be very different from one place to the other, if they are far away from each other. Some countries might be hot, while other countries might be cold. This is one reason why people like to travel to places far away, such as Alaska. Many people visit Alaska to experience something special.

Alaska has a big temperature difference between summer and winter. The hottest temperature recorded was over 37°C. The coldest temperature recorded was -62°C. It can get really cold in Alaska.

Alaska also has a very different time for sunsets from the rest of the world. Sometimes, the sun does not set at all. This is why hotels in Alaska give eye masks to visitors. In some parts of Alaska, the nights can last up to 67 days.

한 지역에서 다른 곳까지는 날씨가 아주 다를 수가 있다. 어떤 나라는 추울 수도 있고 어떤 나라는 더울 수도 있다. 이것은 사람들이 알라스카와 같은 색다른 곳으로 멀리 여행을 떠나고 싶어하는 이유 중 하나이다. 많은 사람들은 특별한 것을 경험하고 싶어서 알라스카를 방문한다.

알라스카는 여름과 겨울의 온도 차가 크다. 가장 더울 때의 온도는 37℃를 넘었고, 가장 추울 때의 온도는 -62℃를 기록하였다. 알라스카는 굉장히 춥다.

알라스카는 또한 일몰시간이 세계의 여타 지역과 매우 다르다. 어떤 때는 태양이 전혀 지지 않는다. 이 때문에 알라스카의 호텔은 투숙객에게 눈가리개를 준다. 알라스카의 어떤 지역에서는 밤이 최고 67일이나 계속되기도 한다.

Listenining Practice ❷   p.95

1. (A)   2. (B)

M: Buildings in US cities are very tall. Are all the tallest buildings of the world in the US?
W: Not really. Many of the tallest buildings are in Asia. The Petronas Twin Towers were once the tallest buildings in the world. They are located in Malaysia.
M: How tall are the towers?
W: They are 452 meters from the ground to the top of the buildings. One of the towers was built by a Korean company.
M: That's interesting. Are they still the tallest buildings in the world?
W: No, the tallest building is now in Taiwan. The building is called Taipei 101, because it has 101 floors.
M: How tall is Taipei 101 compared to the Twin Towers?
W: It is taller by 58 meters. The height of Taipei 101 is 509 meters. It is shaped like a pagoda, and the building is safe from the many earthquakes in Taiwan.

M: 미국의 도시에 있는 건물들은 아주 높아. 가장 높은 건물들은 모두 미국에 있니?
W: 그렇지는 않아. 가장 높은 건물들 중 상당수가 아시아에 있어. Petronas Twin Towers는 한때 세계에서 가장 높은 건물이었어. 그 건물은 말레이시아에 있어.
M: 그 건물은 얼마나 높은데?
W: 땅에서 건물 꼭대기까지 452미터야. 쌍둥이 건물 중 하나는 한국 회사가 지었어.

M: 그거 흥미롭네. 그 건물은 아직도 세계에서 가장 높은 건물이야?
W: 아니, 가장 높은 건물은 지금 대만에 있어. 그 건물은 101층이기 때문에 이름이 Taipei 101이래.
M: Taipei 101은 트윈타워스랑 비교해서 얼마나 높지?
W: 58미터 더 높아. 타이페이 101의 높이는 509미터야. 그 건물은 탑같이 생겼어. 그리고 대만에서 일어나는 잦은 지진으로부터 안전하게 지어졌어.

Listenining Practice ❸   p.96

1. Yes: (B), (D) / No: (A), (C)   2. (C)

W: Hey, I heard you are going somewhere for the holidays.
M: Yes, I'm going to Hollywood this summer with my family.
W: Wow, that's great! What are you planning to do in Hollywood?
M: Oh, they say that there's so much to do and see in Hollywood. My family is going to go on a tour of the whole area.
W: Well, what can you see on the tour?
M: We are going to see the actual studios where famous films are made. The tour also takes us to homes of stars and on a walk down the Hollywood Walk of Fame.
W: Oh, I've seen that street on television. The streets have tiles on the ground in the shape of a star with names of famous people in Hollywood.
M: Yes, I'm looking forward to visiting that street. It will be so different from other streets because there are stars on the ground.

W: 너 휴가 때 어디 간다고 들었는데.
M: 응, 이번 여름에 가족들하고 헐리웃에 갈 거야.
W: 우와, 굉장한데! 헐리웃에서 뭐 할꺼야?
M: 사람들이 그러는데 헐리웃에는 할 것도 볼 것도 많대. 우리 가족은 전 지역을 관광할거야.
W: 어떤 것들을 볼 수 있니?
M: 유명한 영화가 만들어진 실제 스튜디오에 갈 예정이야. 또 유명 배우들의 집에도 가볼 거고 Hollywood Walk of Fame으로 걸어 내려가 보려고 해.
W: 나 텔레비전에서 그 거리 본 적 있어. 그 길에는 헐리웃의 유

명한 사람들 이름이 새겨진 별모양의 타일이 바닥에 깔려 있어.
M: 맞아, 나는 거기에 가기를 고대하고 있어. 걸어 다니면서 땅에 있는 별들을 볼 수도 있기 때문에 다른 거리들과 많이 다를 거 같아.

Listenining Practice ❹   p.97

> 1. (D)   2. (B)

India has a very long history. The country is very big and has the second largest population in the world. This is why there's so much to see.

The Ganges is the longest river in India, and it is considered very holy. While most rivers around the world are for recreation or sports, the Ganges has many other functions. As the Indians believe that the river is holy, people come here to pray and wash themselves in the river. In addition, the river also has thousands of people who wash their clothes by beating them on rocks.

There are many Hindu temples all over India that visitors can enter at any time. The temples are very big and have statues that are thousands of years old. Hinduism is India's main religion, and is similar to Buddhism. Visitors are welcome to eat and sleep in the temple for the night if they have no place to go.

인도는 역사가 매우 오래된 나라다. 인도는 매우 크고, 세계에서 두 번째로 인구가 많은 나라다. 이 때문에 인도에는 볼 것이 많다.

갠지스강은 인도에서 가장 긴 강이고 매우 성스럽게 여겨진다. 대부분의 강이 레크리에이션이나 스포츠의 용도로 이용되는 반면에, 갠지스강은 많은 다른 기능을 가지고 있다. 인도 사람들은 이 강이 신성하다고 여기기 때문에, 이 곳에 와서 기도를 하고 자신들의 몸을 깨끗이 씻기도 한다. 또한 강에서 수천명의 사람들은 돌에 옷을 두드리면서 빨래를 하기도 한다.

인도 전역에는 방문객들이 언제든 들어갈 수 있는 힌두 사원이 많다. 사원들은 매우 크고 몇 천 년이나 된 조각상들이 있다. 힌두교는 인도의 주된 종교이며 불교와 비슷하다. 방문객들은 묵을 곳이 없다면 사원에서 숙식을 할 수 있다.

Listenining Practice ❺   p.98

> 1. (A)   2. (C)

London is visited by many tourists from around the world and is worth visiting at least once. This is because there are so many beautiful things to see in London.

London is home to Big Ben. Many people see the tall clock tower and think that it is Big Ben. However, Big Ben is actually a giant 13 ton bell inside the tower that is rung every hour with a 200 kg hammer. The real name of the bell is the Great Bell of Westminster.

Buckingham Palace is also popular with tourists. It is home to the Queen of England. Tourists enjoy watching the "changing of the guards" ceremony that takes place in front of the palace gates. It is the second largest working palace in the world, after Brunei's "Istana Nurul Iman."

런던은 전세계에서 많은 여행자들이 찾아오고, 한번쯤은 방문해 볼만하다고 여겨지는 곳이다. 왜냐하면 런던에는 아름다운 볼거리들이 많기 때문이다.

런던은 빅벤의 고향이기도 하다. 많은 사람들이 그 커다란 종탑을 보고 그것이 빅벤이라고 생각을 한다. 하지만 사실 빅벤은 매시간마다 200킬로그램의 망치로 울려지는 13톤이나 되는 탑안의 종을 말한다. 그 종의 진짜 이름은 Great Bell of Westminster라고 한다.

버킹엄궁 또한 관광객들에게 인기가 있다. 그곳은 영국여왕의 집이다. 관광객들은 궁문 앞에서 행해지는 근위병 교대식을 보는 것을 아주 좋아한다. 버킹엄궁은 브루나이의 Istana Nurul Iman 다음으로 세계에서 두번째로 큰 실제로 사용되고 있는 궁전이다.

Listenining Practice ❻   p.99

> 1. (D)   2. (C)

The Amazon River in South America is the second longest river in the world, only after the Nile in Africa. The Amazon is over 6,000 km long and is the widest river in the world. There are many animals living in the waters of the Amazon.

The Amazon River has a lot of fish in the water.

Of all the animals that live in the Amazon, a 30 cm fish called the red piranha is king. The red piranha eats meat and hunts for any animal that falls into the water.

Anacondas are the heaviest snakes in the world. Anacondas do not have poison but have very sharp teeth to bite and grab animals. Anacondas can do two things to kill animals: one, drown the animal in the water, and two, crush the animal by squeezing very hard.

남아메리카의 아마존 강은 아프리카의 나일강 다음으로 세계에서 두 번째로 긴 강이다. 아마존 강의 길이는 6,000킬로미터이고 세계에서 가장 넓은 강이다. 아마존 강에는 많은 동물이 살고 있다.

아마존 강에는 많은 종류의 물고기가 산다. 아마존에 사는 동물들 중에서는 30센티미터 크기의 레드 피라나가 왕이다. 레드 피라나는 육류를 먹으며 물 속에 떨어지는 어떤 동물이라도 잡아 먹는다.

아나콘다는 세계에서 가장 무게가 많이 나가는 뱀이다. 아나콘다는 독은 없지만 매우 날카로운 이빨이 있어서 동물을 물고 도망가지 못하게 붙잡는다. 아나콘다가 동물을 죽이기 위해 두 가지 방법을쓰는데, 하나는 물 속에서 익사시키는 것이고, 다른 하나는 아주 강하게 조여서 으깨는 것이다.

iBT Practice 1   p.100

> 1. (B)   2. (D)   3. (B)

Listen to part of a talk in a geography class.

Big rocks are very heavy, so we need a lot of people to move them. This is why Stonehenge in England is such an amazing creation.

The stones in Stonehenge are much heavier than buses. We do not know why people moved the heavy stones to Stonehenge. We do not even know what Stonehenge was used for. Some scientists believe that Stonehenge was used for watching the stars in the sky. This is because the stones seem to follow the pattern of the stars at night.

Others believe that Stonehenge was used as a temple. We don't know if people actually prayed in Stonehenge, but human bones were found in the circle. This made people think that Stonehenge might have been a cemetery at the same time. Perhaps we will never know why or how Stonehenge was built, but it does not matter. Many people still go to see the amazing stones.

큰 바위는 너무 무거워서 그것을 옮기려면 많은 사람의 힘이 필요하다. 이것이 바로 영국의 스톤헨지가 그리도 놀라운 창조물이라 하는 이유다.

스톤헨지의 돌은 버스보다 무겁다. 사람들은 그렇게 무거운 돌이 왜 이곳으로 옮겨졌는지를 알지 못한다. 무슨 용도로 쓰였는지조차도 알지 못한다. 어떤 학자들은 스톤헨지가 하늘의 별을 관측하는 데 쓰였다고 믿는다. 이것은 돌들이 밤에 별들의 움직임을 따라 지어진 것처럼 보이기 때문이다.

다른 학자들은 스톤헨지가 사원으로 사용되었다고 믿기도 한다. 우리는 사람들이 실제로 스톤헨지에서 기도를 했는지는 알 수 없지만, 사람의 뼈가 그곳에서 발견되었다. 이것은 사람들이 스톤헨지가 동시에 무덤으로 이용되었을 수도 있다고 생각하게 했다.

아마도 우리는 왜 그리고 어떻게 스톤헨지가 만들어졌는지 절대 알 수 없을지 모르지만 그것은 중요하지 않다. 여전히 많은 사람들이 그 놀라운 돌들을 보러 간다.

iBT Practice 2   p.102

> 1. Yes: (A), (C) / No: (B), (D)
> 2. (B)   3. (C)

Listen to part of a conversation between two friends.

M: Where are you going for the summer holiday?
W: My family is planning to go to the beach in Thailand.
M: That sounds exciting. What are you planning to do on the beach?
W: Well, I was trying to decide whether I should go scuba diving or snorkeling. My parents said scuba diving is dangerous, so I am going to snorkel. It's safer than scuba diving, and I still get to see the corals.
M: I guess there will be a lot of water sports on the beach as well. People are always trying a new sport there. There are always jet skis for people to ride too.

W: Yes, but I would like to sit on the banana boat. It looks like a lot of fun.
M: That sounds great. What else will you be doing?
W: Oh, I guess I will be eating a lot! Thailand has many types of seafood. I can't wait to be there. I'm so excited!
M: Do me a favor and take many pictures when you're there. I'd really love to see what it's like in Thailand.

M: 이번 여름 휴가에 어디로 갈 거야?
W: 우리 가족은 태국의 해변으로 놀러 갈 예정이야.
M: 재미있겠다. 해변에서 뭘 할 거야?
W: 글쎄, 스쿠버다이빙을 할 건지 스노클링을 할 건지 생각하고 있었어. 부모님이 스쿠버다이빙은 위험하다고 해서 스노클링을 하려고 해. 스쿠버다이빙보다 안전하고 산호도 볼 수 있을 거고.
M: 그밖에 해변에서 할 수 있는 수상스포츠가 많이 있을 것 같은데. 사람들은 언제나 거기서 새로운 스포츠를 시도하더라. 제트스키도 탈 수 있겠구.
W: 응, 그런데 나는 바나나보트를 타고 싶어. 재미있을 거 같아.
M: 그것도 좋은데. 그것 말고 또 뭘 할 거야?
W: 아, 음식도 많이 먹어볼 거야. 태국에는 다양한 해산물이 많아. 기다릴 수가 없네. 너무 신난다!
M: 태국에 가면 사진 좀 많이 찍어와. 태국이 어떤지 굉장히 보고 싶다.

Word Review   p.106

1. lean	2. squeeze
3. drown	4. function
5. cemetery	6. poison
7. pagoda	8. dig
9. in front of	10. look forward to
11. at an angle	12. compared to

Chapter 6
Food
/ Content-Linking

Overview   p.111
Sample Question: (B)

Basic Drills 1   p.112
1. (A)   2. (C)

1. W: What is your favorite food? I love eating seafood.
   M: I prefer steak and other types of meat.
   W: Doctors say that red meat, such as beef, has a lot of cholesterol and fat. We should not eat too much of that.
   M: Well, I guess you're right. Still, I can't help it. I love the taste of steak.

   W: 가장 좋아하는 음식이 뭐니? 나는 해산물을 좋아해.
   M: 나는 스테이크랑 고기 종류를 좋아해.
   W: 의사들이 말하기를 소고기 같은 붉은색 고기에는 콜레스테롤과 지방 함유율이 높대. 많이 먹으면 안 되겠어.
   M: 음, 그런 것 같아. 그렇지만 어쩔 수 없어. 나는 스테이크를 굉장히 좋아하거든.

2. One of the most popular dishes from Italy is spaghetti. But many say that spaghetti is originally from China. Chinese chefs made noodles many years before the Italians, and Italian merchants like Marco Polo brought them back to Italy. Since the vegetables and meat in China were different from those in Italy, the Italians made the noodles into spaghetti.

   이탈리아에서 건너온 가장 대중적인 음식은 스파게티이다. 하지만 많은 사람들이 스파게티가 원래는 중국에서 건너온 것이라고 말을 한다. 중국의 요리사들이 이탈리아 사람들보다 오래전에 면 요리를 만들었고, 마르코 폴로 같은 이탈리아의 상인이 그것을 이탈리아로 가지고 온 것이다. 중국의 야채와 고기가 이탈리아와는 달랐기 때문에 이탈리아인들은 중국의 국수를 스파게티로 만들었다.

Basic Drills 2   p.113

On Your Own

Possible Answer

1. (1) plr bear live extrmly cold ← fur
   (2) invntn pockt wtch → sea travl
   (3) ↓ oxygn & formng storm → dangr climbrs
2. (1) ↑ 100 curry India
   (2) trip amusmnt prk = long & borng
   (3) onin = commn ingrdnt any cultr

2. (1) There are over 100 types of curry in India.
   (2) The trip to the amusement park was very long and boring.
   (3) Onion is the most common ingredient in food of any culture.

Listenining Practice ❶   p.114

1. (B)   2. (C)

Fast food restaurants are everywhere in large cities. This is convenient, and it can taste very good. However, there are some bad things about them.

Some of the ingredients used in fast food restaurants are not very healthy to humans. Foods from these restaurants are usually very high in calories. It would not be so bad if we had regular exercise. But a lot of the people who eat in fast food restaurants are overweight and do not exercise.

Fast foods also lack a proper balanced diet. There are very few vegetables in the menu. If we eat fast food regularly, then we should make sure that we eat vegetables later. Fortunately, many of the fast food companies are introducing salad in their menu. The next time you go into a fast food restaurant, think about getting a salad as well. .

패스트푸드 식당은 대도시 어디에나 있다. 패스트푸드 식당은 편리하고 음식도 대부분 맛이 좋다. 그러나 안좋은 점도 있다.

패스트푸드 식당에서 사용하는 몇몇 음식 재료는 사람들의 건강에 좋지 않다. 음식 대부분은 열량이 높다. 만약 규칙적으로 운동한다면 이것은 크게 나쁘지 않다. 하지만 패스트푸드 식당에서 음식을 먹는 많은 사람들이 과체중이며 운동을 하지 않는다.

또한 패스트푸드는 적절하게 균형 잡힌 식단이 결핍되어 있다. 메뉴를 보면 채소가 거의 없다. 패스트푸드를 정기적으로 먹는다면 나중에 채소를 반드시 먹어야 한다. 다행히 많은 패스트푸드회사들이 메뉴에 샐러드를 도입하고 있다. 다음 번에 패스트푸드 식당에 갈 때에는 샐러드도 같이 곁들여 먹는 것을 생각해라.

Listenining Practice ❷   p.115

1. (A)   2. (C)

A lot of people around the world want to get healthier by eating special foods. In many parts of Asia, they eat some types of food as medicine. A popular food for medicine is called ginseng. There are many types of ginseng.

Ginseng usually grows for 3 to 5 years and is used for many herbal drinks. Ginseng can be grown in many parts of the world, including the US, China, and even France.

Wild oriental ginseng, which only grows in Asia, is expensive and hard to find even in shops. Some people spend a lot of time trying to find it. This type of ginseng takes a much longer time to grow. Some wild ginseng can be over 50 years old.

세계의 많은 사람들이 특별한 식품을 섭취하여 더 건강해지기 원한다. 아시아의 여러 지역에서는 어떤 식품들을 약으로 먹는다. 약으로 인기있는 인삼이라 불리는 식품이 있다. 인삼에는 여러 가지 종류가 있다.

인삼은 보통 3~5년 동안 자라고 다양한 한방차에 이용된다. 인삼은 미국, 중국, 심지어 프랑스 등 세계의 여러 지역에서 재배된다.

아시아 지역에서만 자라는 산삼은 비싸고 가게에서 찾아보기가 어렵다. 어떤 사람들은 많은 시간을 들여 그것을 찾으려 한다. 이 인삼은 자라는데 굉장히 시간이 오래 걸린다. 어떤 산삼은 50년이 넘은 것도 있다.

Listenining Practice ❸   p.116

> 1. (D)   2. Yes: (B), (C) / No: (A), (D)

M: I really enjoy eating Japanese food.
W: That means you prefer eating fish to beef or chicken.
M: How did you know?
W: Most Japanese food is based on fish. The Japanese like to eat a lot of fish. Their favorite food is tuna.
M: Wow, I didn't know that. I just like eating them raw. Are tuna fish expensive?
W: It depends on what type of tuna. The most popular and expensive ones are the giant blue fin tunas. They can reach up to 640 kg. It's a very big fish, and a single tuna can cost over $10,000.
M: That is very expensive. Actually, I prefer eating salmon to tuna in Japanese restaurants.
W: Yes, salmon is another popular dish. But all the salmon that people eat in Japan is imported from other countries, such as Norway and Sweden. Salmon is also often eaten raw or cooked as steak.

M: 나는 일본 음식을 정말 좋아해.
W: 그럼 너는 쇠고기나 닭고기보다 생선을 좋아하겠구나.
M: 어떻게 알았어?
W: 일본 음식 대부분이 생선이 들어가잖아. 일본인은 참 생선을 많이 먹는 것 같아. 가장 좋아하는 음식이 참치래.
M: 와, 그건 몰랐네. 나는 날로 먹는 것을 좋아할 뿐인데. 참치가 비싼 생선인가?
W: 어떤 종류의 참치냐에 따라 다르지. 가장 인기 있고 비싼 것은 giant blue fin 참치야. 무게가 자그마치 640킬로그램이래. 굉장히 큰 생선이지. 참치 한 마리당 10,000달러가 넘는 것도 있어.
M: 정말 비싸네. 사실 나는 일식집에 가면 참치보다 연어를 먹어.
W: 응, 연어는 또 다른 인기 메뉴지. 그렇지만 사람들이 일본에서 먹는 연어는 모두 노르웨이나 스웨덴에서 수입된 것이야. 연어는 종종 날로 먹거나 스테이크처럼 요리해서 먹기도 하지.

Listenining Practice ❹   p.117

> 1. (A)   2. (C)

There are many types of fish in the sea. Some fish are very beautiful, and some look very funny. One type of funny looking fish is called the puffer fish. Puffer fish are eaten mostly by the Japanese and the Koreans.

The puffer fish is one of the most poisonous animals in the world. Yet, many people want to eat this fish. The liver, skin and eggs of the puffer fish contain one of the most dangerous poisons in the world. Only specially trained chefs are allowed to cook the fish in restaurants.

When people eat them raw, the meat is sliced thin enough to actually see through the meat. Some prefer to eat it cooked in soup or porridge. Whatever way people like to eat it, puffer fish is very expensive and perhaps too dangerous to eat.

바다에는 많은 종류의 물고기가 산다. 어떤 것은 매우 아름답고 어떤 것은 매우 우스꽝스럽게 생겼다. 그런 물고기 중에 복어가 있다. 복어는 주로 일본인과 한국인이 먹는다.

복어는 세계에서 가장 독성이 강한 동물 중 하나이다. 그러나 많은 사람들이 복어를 먹고 싶어한다. 복어의 간, 껍질, 그리고 알에는 세상에서 가장 무서운 독이 들어있다. 숙련된 요리사만이 음식점에서 복어를 요리할 수 있도록 되어 있다.

복어를 날로 먹을 때는 비쳐 보일 정도로 얇게 썬다. 어떤 사람들은 수프나 죽으로 만들어 먹기도 한다. 어떤 방법으로 먹든지 복어요리는 비싸고 먹기에 너무 위험하다.

Listenining Practice ❺   p.118

> 1. (A)   2. (B)

W: I can't wait to celebrate Thanksgiving. I am planning to make a very tasty roast turkey.
M: Why are you cooking turkey on Thanksgiving?
W: Nearly everyone in the US eats roasted turkey during Thanksgiving. It is a holiday to remember the first meal between the Pilgrims and the Indians in America.
M: Oh, I see. The Chinese people also make special food during holidays.

W: Really? I didn't know that.
M: Yes, the Chinese celebrate the Full Moon Festival by making desserts called moon cakes. This day is also Thanksgiving Day in Korea.
M: What is moon cake?
W: Moon cakes are mostly enjoyed by the Chinese during the festival. They are like sweet bread, filled with many different things. Long ago, the Chinese used to put secret messages inside the cakes when Mongols ruled China.

W: 추수감사절이 기다려지는걸. 아주 맛있는 칠면조 구이를 만들어보려고 해.
M: 왜 추수감사절에 칠면조를 요리하는 거니?
W: 미국에 있는 거의 모든 사람이 추수감사절에 구운 칠면조를 먹지. 추수감사절은 미대륙의 인디언들과 청교도들이 함께 한 첫 식사를 기리기 위한 거야.
M: 아, 그렇구나. 중국인들도 명절 때 특별한 음식을 만들어 먹어.
W: 정말? 몰랐어.
M: 중국인은 월병이라고 불리는 후식을 만들어서 추석을 축하해. 이 날은 한국의 추석과 같지.
M: 월병이 뭐야?
W: 월병은 중국 사람들이 명절 때 주로 즐기는 음식이야. 달콤한 빵 같고, 속은 여러 다른 것들로 채워져 있어. 옛날에 중국 사람들은 몽고가 중국을 지배했을 때 월병 속에 비밀 전갈을 넣어 전달하곤 했대.

Listenining Practice 6 p.119

1. (D)   2. (B)

Ice cream is the most popular dessert in the world. There are many stories about how it became popular. The stories might not be true because they do not say how ice cream was actually made.

One story says that ice cream was invented in the 1600s. A chef made the first ice cream for King Charles I of England. The king was so fond of eating the ice cream that he paid the chef a lot of money to keep it a secret. In 1649, King Charles I was killed, and the chef told everyone about the ice cream.

There is also another story that says how Marco Polo ate ice cream when he was in China, and brought the recipe back to Italy in the 1200s. Then, one Italian princess married a prince from another country, and that's how some think ice cream became popular.

아이스크림은 세계에서 가장 인기 있는 후식이다. 아이스크림이 어떻게 널리 퍼졌는가에 대해서는 많은 이야기가 있다. 그 이야기들은 아이스크림이 실제로 어떻게 만들어졌는지에 대해서는 말하고 있지 않기 때문에 사실이 아닐지도 모른다.

아이스크림이 1600년대에 만들어졌다고 하는 이야기가 있다. 영국의 찰스 1세를 위해 한 요리사가 처음으로 아이스크림을 만들었다. 왕은 아이스크림을 너무 좋아해서 아이스크림을 비밀로 하도록 요리사에게 많은 돈을 주었다. 1649년에 찰스 1세가 죽자 요리사는 모든 사람에게 아이스크림에 대해 말했다.

다른 이야기에 따르면 마르코 폴로가 중국에 있을 때 아이스크림을 먹고 1200년대에 이탈리아로 돌아올 때 그 제조법을 들여왔다고 한다. 그 후 이탈리아 공주 하나가 다른 나라의 왕자와 결혼하여 아이스크림이 널리 퍼졌다는 것이다.

iBT Practice 1 p.120

1. (C)   2. (D)   3. (A)

Listen to part of a talk in a classroom.

Some countries enjoy eating food that other countries do not eat at all. Here are some countries with very different ideas of what food is.

In Texas, U.S.A., there's a festival for rattlesnake meat. The meat is coated in flour and fried in very hot oil. It is a very popular dish in Texas, and some of the people say that rattlesnake meat is the most delicious in the world.

Small shops in the streets of Thailand sell fried bats. The bat is fried whole, so that people can still see the bat wings and head on it. It is not very cheap, because it is hard to catch the bats.

The people in France eat what is known as foie gras, meaning fat liver. The liver mostly comes from ducks, although it was originally from geese. The farmers force the ducks to eat a lot of corn for 4 to 5 months. This makes the liver really big. Many people want this to stop, because they say that the ducks suffer a lot.

한 나라에서는 전혀 먹지 않는 음식을 어떤 나라에서는 즐겨 먹는다. 여기서 음식이라는 것에 대해 각기 다른 생각을 갖고 있는 나라들을 살펴보자.

미국의 텍사스에서는 방울뱀고기 축제가 있다. 뱀고기에 밀가루를 입혀 고온의 기름에 튀긴다. 이 요리는 텍사스에서 매우 인기있는 음식이다. 이곳의 어떤 사람들은 세상에서 방울뱀고기가 제일 맛있다고 한다.

태국의 거리에 있는 작은 상점에서는 박쥐튀김을 판다. 박쥐를 통째로 튀겨서 박쥐의 날개와 그 위에 달린 머리까지 볼 수 있다. 박쥐를 잡는 것이 어렵기 때문에 가격은 그다지 싸지 않다.

프랑스 사람들은 지방간을 의미하는 후아그라라고 알려진 음식을 먹는다. 이 간은 원래 거위에서 나오는 것이지만 대부분은 오리의 간이다. 농부들이 4내지 5개월 동안 거위에게 엄청난 양의 옥수수를 먹이는데 이렇게 해서 간을 크게 만든다. 거위가 고통스러워하기 때문에 많은 사람들이 이를 금지하게끔 하기를 원한다.

iBT Practice 2
p.122

1. (D)   2. Yes: (A), (D) / No: (B), (C)
3. (C)

Listen to part of a conversation between two friends.

M: Look at what I bought from the store today. It's yak's milk.

W: Yak? What's that?

M: It's a kind of cow. Well, they aren't really cows that people see in milk farms. Yaks are big animals that live mostly in colder regions in Asia, such as Nepal and parts of China. They are used for carrying heavy things across mountains.

W: Wow, I didn't know that. Why did you buy yak's milk?

M: 🎧 **A lot of people think eating food from a strong animal makes you healthier. The one bad point is that the taste might be too strong for some people.**

W: Well, I have tried goat's milk, and I'm crazy about it. It was very tasty. I think goat's milk is sweeter than cow's milk. I think I'll get myself a bottle of goat's milk tomorrow.

M: Oh yeah. Goat's milk is very popular too. A lot of people in India drink goat's milk. Indians think that goat's milk can cure many illnesses, so many sick people drink goat's milk as medicine. But again, not everyone likes goat's milk.

M: 오늘 내가 가게에서 산 것 좀 봐. 야크 우유야.

W: 야크? 그게 뭐야?

M: 소의 일종이야. 야크는 사람들이 우유 농장에서 보는 일반 소가 아니야. 네팔이나 중국 일부 지역처럼 주로 아시아의 추운 지방에서 사는 큰 동물이지. 무거운 짐을 지고 산을 넘는데 이용해.

W: 우와, 몰랐네. 야크 우유는 왜 샀어?

M: 많은 사람들이 강한 동물에서 나온 음식을 먹으면 더 건강해진다고 생각해. 하나 안좋은 점은 어떤 사람에게는 그 우유 맛이 너무 강할지도 모른다는 것이야.

W: 음, 나는 염소 우유를 먹어본 적이 있는데 아주 좋아하게 됐어. 굉장히 맛있었어. 내 생각에 염소 우유는 소우유보다 조금 단 것 같아. 내일은 염소 우유 한 병을 사야겠군.

M: 그래, 염소 우유도 매우 인기 있지. 많은 인도 사람들이 염소 우유를 마셔. 인도 사람들은 염소 우유가 병을 낫게 한다고 믿어서 많은 아픈 사람들이 약으로 염소 우유를 마신대. 그런데 염소 우유도 모든 사람들이 좋아하는건 아니야.

Word Review
p.126

1. overweight	2. vegetarian
3. import	4. raw
5. region	6. regularly
7. convenience	8. recipe
9. depend on	10. including
11. up to	12. is based on

Chapter 7
Art & Entertainment
/ Stance / Attitude

Overview　　　　　　　　　　p.131

Sample Question: (D)

Basic Drills 1　　　　　　　　p.132

1. (C)　　2. (B)

1. The oldest pictures in the world are paintings on cave walls. They were drawn thousands of years ago by people that lived in the caves. They drew pictures of animals and how they hunted for them. It was great that we found the drawings, as the pictures helped professors understand how they lived.

   세상에서 가장 오래된 그림은 동굴벽화이다. 동굴벽화는 수천 년 전에 동굴에서 살았던 사람들이 그렸다. 그들은 동물을 그렸고 어떻게 동물을 사냥했는지를 그려놓았다. 이것은 학자들이 그 당시 사람들의 생활 모습을 이해하는데 도움을 주었기 때문에 벽화가 발견된 것은 굉장한 일이었다.

2. M: Did you know that the painting of Mona Lisa does not have eyebrows?
   W: Are you sure? I've seen it many times on television, but I didn't notice.
   M: It's true. Moreover, some also say that the woman in the picture might not even be smiling. That's why some call her the lady with the mysterious smile.

   M: 모나리자 그림을 보면 눈썹이 없다는 거 알아?
   W: 정말이야? 그 그림 텔레비전에서 여러 번 봤는데 몰랐는걸.
   M: 맞아. 게다가 어떤 사람들은 그림 속의 여자가 미소 짓고 있는 게 아니라고 말해. 그게 사람들이 그 여자를 불가사의한 미소를 가진 여인이라고 부르는 이유지.

Basic Drills 2　　　　　　　　p.133

On Your Own

1. We must remember the three rules of soccer. First, we must not touch the ball with our hands. Second, the ball must not go out of the white line. Third, we must start in the middle of the field after we score a goal.
2. because of, First, Second

2. The cheetah is the fastest animal in the world. It can run quickly because of two things. First, the cheetah's legs are very powerful. They can push the cheetah to run nearly 80 km/h. Second, the cheetah's tail gives the animal very good balance when it runs. Without its tail, the cheetah would probably fall.

Listenining Practice ❶　　　　p.134

1. (B)　　2. (D)

When people talk about picture art, they think about paintings with brush on paper. However, art can be drawn on anything. As long as the artists are expressing themselves, it can be called art.

There are some artists who draw on cars. People pay a lot of money to get their cars painted by special painters. A lot of the paintings on cars are drawings of fire. Most of the work looks wonderful and really special.

Tattoo artists "draw" on humans by using a special needle machine. The machine has ink on the tip of the needles. There are many famous tattoo artists, as more people around the world want tattoos. Tattoos done by famous artists can look very artistic and colorful.

사람들이 미술에 대해 이야기할 때 종이에 붓으로 그린 그림만 생각한다. 하지만 미술 작품은 어떤 것에나 그려질 수 있다. 작가가 자신을 표현하기만 한다면 그것은 예술이라고 할 수 있다.

자동차에 그림을 그리는 예술가가 있다. 사람들은 자신의 자동차에 특별한 화가의 그림을 그리게 하려고 많은 돈을 지불한다. 자동차에 그리는 많은 그림은 불을 소재로 그린다. 작품 대부분이 다 놀랍고 정말 특별하게 보인다.

문신 아티스트는 특수한 바늘 기계를 사용해서 사람의 몸에 그림을 그린다. 기계 끝에는 잉크가 묻은 바늘이 달려있다. 세계 곳곳의 사람들이 문신을 하고 싶어함에 따라 유명한 문신 아티스트도 많이 있다. 유명한 아티스트가 새긴 문신은 정말 예술적이고 다채롭기까지 하다.

Listenining Practice ❷ p.135

1. (C)   2. (C)

There are many ways that performers can express themselves to others, sometimes without even saying a word.

There are many performers called mimes in the US and Europe. These people paint their faces like clowns and make people laugh. The differences between clowns and mimes are that mimes do not speak at all, and they neither use toys nor tools. They only use their actions to let people understand what they are trying to express.

Another good performance is the one-man band. One-man bands have all sorts of musical instruments stuck on their bodies. When they move their bodies, it will either hit or play an instrument. They are fun and entertaining to watch. Unfortunately, one-man band performers are disappearing.

예술가들이 자기를 표현하는데 여러 방법이 있다. 때로는 아무 말도 하지 않기도 한다.

미국과 유럽에는 마임이라고 불리는 공연자가 많이 있다. 이들은 얼굴을 광대처럼 분장하여 사람들을 웃긴다. 광대와 마임 간의 차이는 마임은 전혀 대사가 없고 장난감이나 도구를 사용하지 않는다는 것이다. 마임은 사람들에게 공연자가 표현하고자 하는 바를 이해시키기 위해 몸동작만을 사용한다.

또 다른 공연으로는 1인 밴드가 있다. 1인 밴드는 한 사람의 몸에 온갖 종류의 악기가 붙어있는 것이다. 한번 몸을 움직이면 악기가 쳐지거나 연주가 된다. 그것을 보면 재미있고 즐겁다. 안타깝게도 1인 밴드 연주자들이 점차 사라져가고 있다.

Listenining Practice ❸ p.136

1. (A)   2. (C)

W: Have you seen the paintings by Picasso in the museum? I didn't think they were that great.
M: Really? I think his paintings are wonderful. He is a genius.
W: I am not sure if he is a genius. I mean, it's so hard to understand what he is trying to say in the paintings.
M: I think that is exactly what he wanted. Picasso created art called cubism, and the meaning should not be easy to understand.
W: I see. Well, some might call him a great painter, but I prefer Monet. His drawings are clear and easy to understand. I hope I can buy his paintings one day.
M: That's art. It should either be easy or hard to understand. One drawing can't be good for everyone. I guess that's why they say, "Beauty lies in the eye of the beholder."

W: 박물관에서 피카소 그림 본 적 있어? 그렇게 굉장하다는 생각은 안 들더라.
M: 그래? 나는 멋있다고 생각하는데. 그 사람은 천재야.
W: 난 피카소가 천재인 줄 모르겠어. 내 말은 그 사람이 그림에서 말하고자 하는 것을 이해하는 게 너무 어렵다는 거야.
M: 나는 그게 바로 피카소가 원한 거라고 생각해. 피카소는 입체파라고 하는 예술을 창조했고, 그 의미를 이해하기란 쉬운 게 아니야.
W: 알겠어. 어떤 사람들은 피카소를 위대한 화가라고 할 지도 모르겠지만 나는 모네가 더 좋아. 그 사람의 작품은 이해하기 쉽고 분명하지. 나중에 그 사람의 작품을 살 수 있다면 좋겠어.
M: 그게 예술이지. 이해하기 쉽거나 혹은 이해하기 어렵다는 것. 한 작품이 모든 사람에게 좋은 작품이 되는 건 아니거든. 그래서 사람들이 '제눈에 안경이다'라고 하는가 봐.

Listenining Practice ❹ p.137

1. (B)   2. (C)

Photography is gaining a lot of popularity among many people as a way to express themselves. It is enjoyed by many people as a type of hobby, and there are two main reasons why this is happening.

It is easy to start photography, as all a beginner needs is a camera. In fact, it is now even easier to start photography, thanks to digital cameras. We neither need dangerous chemicals to develop the film nor wait for it to dry.

We can get a lot of information about photography on the internet. The internet is filled with professional photographers. They can give us good advice about taking pictures. I guess the only hard part about photography is the cost of the camera itself!

사진 촬영은 자기자신을 표현하는 하나의 방법으로 사람들 사이에서 인기를 얻고 있다. 많은 사람들이 취미로 즐기는데, 이러한 현상이 일어나는 데는 두가지 이유가 있다.

초보자에게 필요한 것은 카메라뿐이기 때문에 쉽게 사진을 시작할 수 있다. 사실, 디지털카메라 덕분에 사진을 시작하는 것은 이제 훨씬 더 쉬워졌다. 필름을 인화하기 위해 위험한 화학물질을 다루거나 사진이 마를 때까지 기다릴 필요가 없다.

사진 촬영에 대한 많은 정보를 인터넷에서 구할 수도 있다. 인터넷은 전문 사진작가들로 가득하다. 그들은 사진 촬영에 대해 좋은 조언을 제공한다. 예술로서 사진의 어려운 점은 카메라의 가격밖에 없다고 본다!

Listenining Practice ❺   p.138

1. (D)   2. (C)

T: 🎧 What are some types of art that you have heard of?
M: What do you mean? Isn't art just paintings?
W: No, there are also statues. I think they are great.
T: Yes, statues are art pieces too. There are so many more types of art as well. Art is basically anything that can be used to express yourself.
W: In that case, can dancing also be considered art? I enjoy dancing a lot.
M: I think it should be called art. When people dance, they are expressing themselves by moving to the music.
T: You're absolutely right. Dancing can definitely be called art. In fact, it is called a performing art. Drama, singing, dancing, all these are performing arts.
W: Oh, so that's why singers are called artists. When I was young, I didn't understand why singers were called artists.
M: That's funny. I didn't know either.
T: 예술 분야에 대해 무엇인가를 들어 본 적이 있니?
M: 그게 무슨 뜻이죠? 예술에는 그림만 있는 거 아닌가요?
W: 아니야, 조각도 있어. 조각분야도 굉장해.
T: 맞아. 조각도 예술 작품 중 하나란다. 그것 말고도 다른 종류의 예술이 굉장히 많지. 기본적으로 예술은 자기 자신을 표현할 수 있는 것을 말한단다.
M: 그렇게 말씀하시면, 춤도 예술이 될 수 있는 건가요? 저는 춤을 굉장히 좋아하는데요.
W: 내 생각엔 될 수 있는 거 같아. 무용가들이 춤을 출때 음악에 맞춰 움직이면서 자신을 표현하잖아.
T: 맞아. 무용도 분명히 예술이라 할 수 있어. 사실, 무용은 공연예술이라고 불리지. 드라마, 노래, 무용 이 모든 것이 공연예술에 속해.
W: 오, 그래서 가수를 예술가라고 부르는 거군요. 나는 왜 가수들이 예술가라고 불리는지 이해가 안갔었어요.
M: 그거 재미있네. 나도 그랬었는데.

Listenining Practice ❻   p.139

1. (D)   2. (B)

Clown are popular with almost everyone in the world. Clown are found either in places where there are children or people, and clowns work hard to entertain them. This is why there are clown universities in the US to train the clowns to be the best clowns in the world.

Clown universities teach students how to act properly. Since most clowns do not speak in shows, they must make sure that their actions on stage look very funny. 🎧 Everyone likes a funny clown, and the university makes sure that the clowns know how to make people laugh.

Clown universities also teach students how to paint their faces. Clowns often spend many hours on stage, and if their face is not painted properly, the makeup will not look good. This is why clowns often spend hours in front of the mirror to draw on their face.

광대는 세계 모든 사람들에게 인기가 있다. 어린 아이들이나 사람들이 모이는 곳에서는 광대를 찾아 볼 수 있고, 그들은 사람들을 즐겁게 해주기 위해 열심히 노력한다. 이 때문에 미국에는 세계 제일의 광대를 훈련시키는 광대 학교가 있다.

광대 학교는 학생들에게 적절하게 행동하는 법을 가르친다. 쇼에서 광대는 대부분 말을 하지 않기 때문에 무대에서의 행동이 아주 웃기게 보이도록 해야 한다. 누구나 웃긴 광대를 좋아하므로 광대 학교는 광대가 어떻게 사람들을 웃길 것인지 가르친다.

광대 학교는 또한 학생들에게 얼굴 분장법도 가르친다. 광대는 무대에서 여러 시간을 보내고, 얼굴을 제대로 분장하지 않으면 얼굴이 이상하게 보일 것이다. 광대가 얼굴을 분장하기 위해 종종 거울 앞에서 몇 시간을 보내는 이유가 여기에 있다.

*i*BT Practice ①   p.140

1. Yes: (A), (D) / No: (B), (C)
2. (D)   3. (A)

Listen to part of a conversation between two friends.

M: I heard that a famous magician is coming to school today.
W: Yes, that is correct. I saw his show about a month ago on television. He is very good with magic tricks.
M: Really? I love to watch magic shows. I know they are only tricks, but I still enjoy watching things disappear in the magician's hands. It's amazing what they can do.
W: I agree with you. They always have so much fun entertaining people with their wonderful tricks.
M: Yes, I even thought about becoming a magician when I was younger. 🎧 **I wish I could do some tricks of my own. I read a book about magic some time ago. Some tricks looked really easy, but most of them looked really hard to do.**
W: That is because it takes years of practice to be a very good magician. Not everyone can do magic tricks as easily as magicians can. Anyway, I guess I'll see you at the show later. I have to go to class now.

M: 유명한 마술사가 오늘 학교에 온다고 들었어.
W: 그래, 맞아. 텔레비전에서 그 사람의 쇼를 한달 전에 본 적이 있어. 아주 마술을 잘 하더라.
M: 정말? 난 마술 보는 거 무지 좋아해. 마술이 속임수에 불과하다는 걸 알지만 손에서 물건이 사라지는 걸 보는 것은 여전히 즐거워. 마술사들이 하는 마술은 참 신기해.
W: 동감이야. 언제나 사람들을 놀라운 기술로 즐겁게 해주는 재미가 있잖아.
M: 그래, 나는 어렸을 때에는 마술사가 될까 하고 생각했을 정도였거든. 나도 몇 가지 기술을 배우고 싶어. 얼마 전에 마술에 대한 책을 읽었어. 어떤 기술은 굉장히 쉬워 보였는데, 대부분은 정말 어려워 보이더라.
W: 그래서 훌륭한 마술사가 되는데 수년간의 연습이 필요한 거야. 모든 사람이 마술사처럼 쉽게 마술을 할 수 있는 건 아니거든. 어쨌든 나중에 마술 쇼에서 보자. 난 지금 수업에 들어가야 돼.

*i*BT Practice ②   p.142

1. (C)   2. (B)   3. (D)

Listen to part of a conversation between two students and a teacher.

T: We'll be talking about Shakespeare today. Does anyone know who he is?
M: He was a famous writer that wrote many story books.
W: He didn't write story books. He wrote plays.
T: Yes, very good. He was a writer that wrote plays during the 16th century. Many think of him as a genius.
W: I certainly agree that he is a genius. His plays are wonderful. His most famous play, *Romeo and Juliet*, is still what people remember when they think about romance.
M: I read some of his plays, but they were so hard to understand. They didn't look like they were in English. I nearly gave up reading halfway. I don't think I will read any more of his plays.
T: That's because they were written long ago, and the English language was a little bit different

back then. For example, "thy" meant your, and "thou" meant you. Once you get used to it, it's not too difficult to understand it.

W: It was hard for me too, but I made a list of words. It might not work for everyone, but it helped me understand the play better. You should give Shakespeare another chance.

M: Yes, maybe I should do that.

T: 오늘은 셰익스피어에 대해서 얘기해 보려고 한다. 셰익스피어가 누구인지 아는 사람 있니?

M: 셰익스피어는 많은 이야기책을 쓴 유명한 작가예요.

W: 이야기책을 쓴 게 아니라 희곡을 썼어.

T: 그래, 아주 잘 대답했어. 셰익스피어는 16세기에 희곡을 쓴 작가란다. 많은 사람들이 그를 천재라고 하지.

W: 그 사람은 정말 천재라고 생각해요. 그 사람의 희곡은 놀라워요. 가장 유명한 희곡인 <로미오와 줄리엣>은 아직도 사람들이 로맨스 하면 떠올리는 작품이죠.

M: 셰익스피어의 희곡을 몇 개 읽어보았지만 이해하기가 너무 어려웠어요. 영어로 쓰여진 것 같지 않았거든요. 반쯤 읽다가 거의 포기했어요. 저는 앞으로 셰익스피어의 희곡은 더 못 읽을 거 같아요.

T: 그건 그것들이 옛날에 쓰여졌고 영어 표현이 당시에는 조금 달랐기 때문이란다. 예를 들어서 "thy"는 '당신의'를, "thou"는 '당신'을 뜻하는 말이지. 한번 익숙해지면 이해하는데 그다지 어려움이 없을 거야.

W: 나도 어려웠는데 단어 목록을 만들어 봤어. 단어 목록이 모든 사람들한테 효과가 있을지는 모르지만, 그것이 내가 셰익스피어 희곡을 더 잘 이해하는데 도움이 되었어. 너도 셰익스피어를 다시 읽어 보도록 해봐.

M: 좋아, 아무래도 그래야겠네.

Word Review p.146

1. disappear	2. entertaining
3. expert	4. tattoo
5. trick	6. instrument
7. develop	8. chemical
9. thanks to	10. get used to
11. as well	12. is filled with

Chapter 8
Social Issues
/ Function-Purpose

Overview p.151
Sample Question: (C)

Basic Drills 1 p.152
1. (B)   2. (A)

1. W: Did you hear that more subjects might be added in school?

M: What? That's impossible. We already have many subjects to study, and there's not enough time for them all.

W: Yes, I agree with you. I think we learn too many subjects already. I wish people knew that students have a really hard time in school with studies.

W: 학교 교과목이 더 늘어날지도 모른다는 얘기 들었어?

M: 뭐? 말도 안돼. 공부할 게 벌써 굉장히 많잖아. 그리고 그걸 다 할 시간도 없다구.

W: 응, 나도 그렇게 생각해. 이미 너무 많은 과목을 배우고 있어. 학생들이 학교에서 공부하느라 얼마나 힘든 시간을 보내고 있는지 사람들이 알았으면 좋겠어.

2. Drunk driving is a big problem all over the world. People cannot make quick decisions and feel sleepy when they drink alcohol. They are dangerous to themselves and also to others on the road. People are not keeping quiet about drunk driving anymore.

음주 운전은 세계적으로 큰 문제다. 술을 마시면 사람들은 판단을 빨리 할 수 없고 졸음이 오게 된다. 이것은 자기자신과 길 위의 다른 사람들에게도 위험하다. 사람들은 음주운전자에 대해 더 이상은 침묵을 지키지만은 않는다.

Basic Drills 2 p.153

On Your Own

1. People use the internet to find a lot of information. <u>However</u>, finding the correct information can be very difficult. <u>Therefore</u>, it would be helpful to know a few tips. Use the plus sign if it is a keyword and a minus sign if you do not want the results to have that certain word. You can <u>also</u> use a question mark <u>if</u> you are not sure of the spelling.
2. Therefore, if, also, If, then

2. Many people use the subway to travel around a city. <u>Therefore</u>, we should always be polite to others in the subway. We should be quiet if we are talking on the phone or with another person. We should <u>also</u> give our seat to old people and pregnant women. <u>If</u> we are listening to music, <u>then</u> we should play it softly.

Listenining Practice 1 p.154

1. (D)   2. (B)

People around the world always look for new ways to save the environment. Keeping the earth clean all the time is an important part of our lives. There are a few things we should always remember.

We must always remember not to waste the important things in life. Only 1% of the water in the world is drinking water, so we must be careful to use only a little. Paper and tissue come from trees, and we should make sure we do not waste them.

Recycling is also very important. Thanks to new technology, we can reuse many things in our daily lives. Paper and plastic products are the most used items in the world, and we can recycle both of them. We should always remember to put them in the recycle bins.

세상 사람들은 환경을 보존하기 위해 언제나 새로운 방법을 강구한다. 지구를 항상 깨끗하게 유지하는 것은 우리 삶을 위한 중요한 부분이다. 이에 우리가 항상 기억해야 할 몇 가지가 있다.

우리는 생활 속에서 중요한 것들을 낭비해서는 안된다는 것을 명심해야 한다. 지구상의 1%의 물만이 식수이다. 그러므로 조금씩 사용하도록 주의해야 한다. 종이와 화장지는 나무로 만드는데 이들 또한 낭비하지 않도록 해야 한다.

또한 재활용도 매우 중요하다. 새로운 기술 덕분에 우리는 일상 생활에서 많은 것들을 다시 사용할 수 있다. 종이와 플라스틱 제품은 가장 많이 쓰이는 품목이며, 둘 다 재활용할 수 있다. 재활용 수거함에 그것들을 넣는 것을 언제나 명심해야 한다.

Listenining Practice 2 p.155

1. (C)   2. (B)

W: Don't you think that there are too many buses on the streets? I can't get anywhere on time anymore with my car.
M: I think it's great that they increased the number of buses. You should use the bus or the subway. Public transportation seems to be the best, if you want to get anywhere on time.
W: But I want to sit when I'm traveling, and I can't seem to find a seat. I'm always standing in buses. It's the same in the subway as well. It's so crowded in subways.
M: 🎧 Yes, it's a little inconvenient, but you had better take the bus as there are bus lanes now. It's much cheaper than driving around as well. You don't even need to park your car.
W: **Yes, I'm with you there.** I guess I'll start taking the bus tomorrow.

W: 길에 버스가 너무 많다고 생각하지 않아? 어디를 가도 더 이상 차로는 제시간에 갈 수 없어.
M: 나는 버스 수를 늘린 것은 좋은 생각이라고 봐. 버스나 지하철을 이용해봐. 어디를 갈 때 시간을 맞춰서 가고 싶다면 대중 교통이 가장 좋은 것 같아.
W: 하지만 돌아다닐 때 앉아서 가고 싶은데 빈 자리가 없잖아. 항상 버스에서 서서 간다구. 그건 지하철도 마찬가지야. 지하철에는 사람이 정말 많아.
M: 맞아, 좀 불편하지. 그렇지만 이제는 버스 전용 차선이 있기 때문에 정시에 도착하려면 버스를 타는게 좋을 거야. 게다가 운전하는 것보다 돈이 훨씬 덜 들어. 차를 주차시킬 필요도

없지.
W: 맞아, 그건 나도 같은 생각이야. 내일부터는 버스를 타기 시작해야겠다.

Listenining Practice ❸ p.156

1. (A)   2. (C)

A lot of people spend time doing volunteer work. Some volunteers choose to help in keeping the environment clean, and some choose to help other people. There have been more volunteers recently, and there are many ways to become a volunteer.

For instance, there are many volunteers on the highways of the US. They even have programs like "Adopt-A-Highway" that put a kilometer of highway under someone's care. The person would be responsible for cleaning and keeping that area beautiful.

🎧 **The easiest type of volunteer work that helps other people is donating blood. All that a person needs to do is to lie down,** and the nurses will take a little bit of blood from the person's arm. Hospitals always need a lot of blood, so we should always donate blood when we can.

많은 사람들이 자원 봉사를 하는데 시간을 할애한다. 어떤 자원 봉사자는 환경을 깨끗하게 보존하는 것을 돕기 위해서, 어떤 자원 봉사자는 다른 사람을 돕는 봉사 활동을 한다. 요즘에는 점점 자원 봉사자가 많아지고, 자원 봉사자가 되는데도 여러 가지 방법이 있다.

예를들어, 미국의 고속도로에는 자원 봉사자가 많이 있다. 미국에는 "Adopt-A-Highway"(고속도로에서 쓰레기를 없애기 위한 캠페인) 같은 프로그램이 있어서 고속도로 1킬로미터마다 각자의 구간을 관리하게 하고 있다. 그 사람은 책임감을 갖고 맡은 구역을 깨끗이 하고 아름답게 보존한다.

다른 사람을 돕는 자원 봉사 활동 중 가장 쉬운 것은 헌혈이다. 그냥 누워있으면 된다. 그러면 간호사가 팔에서 어느 정도의 피를 뽑을 것이다. 병원은 항상 많은 양의 피를 필요로 한다. 그러므로 할 수 있다면 우리는 언제나 헌혈을 해야 한다.

Listenining Practice ❹ p.157

1. (B)   2. (D)

W: Do you throw away rubbish properly in recycle bins?
M: Of course. I always make sure that I throw plastic and paper in the proper bins. Why do you ask?
W: Well, I only started recycling recently. I didn't know it was that important.
M: You should always remember to recycle. It's not very hard to throw away plastic and paper into the proper recycle bins. By recycling, we can really make a lot of difference in the environment.
W: 🎧 Yes, I read in the newspapers last week that recycling can really help the environment. That is why I've been more careful to recycle my rubbish properly.
M: **I think you made the right choice.** Do you also throw glass in the recycle bin?
W: Yes, I make sure that all my bottles and cans also get recycled.

W: 너는 재활용 수거함에 쓰레기를 제대로 버리니?
M: 물론. 나는 언제나 맞는 통에 플라스틱과 종이를 버리는지 확인을 해. 그런데 왜 물어보는 거야?
W: 어, 나는 요즘에야 재활용을 시작했거든. 그게 그렇게 중요한 줄 몰랐어.
M: 항상 재활용하는 걸 명심해야해. 플라스틱이랑 종이를 맞는 통에 버리는 건 그렇게 어렵지 않아. 재활용을 함으로써 우리는 환경에 엄청난 차이를 만들 수 있어.
W: 맞아, 나는 지난 주에 재활용이 환경 보호를 돕는다고 신문에서 읽었어. 그게 내가 쓰레기를 제대로 버리는 것에 좀더 신경 쓰게 된 이유야.
M: 옳은 선택이라고 생각해. 재활용 수거함에 유리도 버리니?
W: 응, 유리병하고 캔도 재활용될 수 있도록 항상 확인하고 있어.

Listenining Practice ❺ p.158

1. (C)   2. (B)

Many parents are sending their children overseas for education. Some parents send their children to boarding schools, or the children can stay with another family.

Boarding schools are schools with bedrooms for students to study and sleep. Boarding schools are usually very expensive, and their system is very strict. The schools teach the children how to live with other students. Many students do not like going to boarding schools at first, but most like the freedom away from their parents.

Homestay can also be a great experience. Homestay is staying with another family in a different country. It allows the children to learn about independence as well as a different culture. Some children can feel homesick, but most enjoy it later.

많은 부모들이 교육을 위해 아이들을 해외로 유학을 보낸다. 어떤 부모는 아이들을 기숙학교로 보내기도 하고 아니면 다른 가족과 함께 지내게 하기도 한다.

기숙 학교는 학생들이 공부하고 잠잘 수 있는 침실을 제공하는 학교이다. 기숙 학교는 대체로 비싸고 교육체계가 엄격하다. 학교는 아이들에게 다른 학생들과 함께 살아가는 방법을 가르친다. 많은 학생들이 처음에 기숙 학교에 가는 것을 좋아하지 않지만, 대부분 부모로부터 떨어져있을 수 있는 자유를 좋아한다.

홈스테이 또한 좋은 경험이 될 수 있다. 홈스테이는 다른 나라에서 모르는 가족과 함께 지내는 것을 말한다. 아이들이 다른 문화는 물론 독립심을 배우게 해준다. 간혹 향수병에 걸릴 수도 있지만 시간이 지나면 대부분 즐거워한다.

Listenining Practice 6 p.159

1. (A)   2. (C)

W: Cigarette prices have gone up again.
M: That's good to hear. People should not be smoking anyway. It's so bad for our health.
W: I know, but so many people still smoke.
M: They really should quit smoking. There's nothing good about it.
W: Well, smokers say that cigarettes relieve stress and help them calm down.
M: 🎧 It's not the cigarettes at all. It's the time that they take to smoke. The cigarette has nothing to do with calming them down.
W: Really? I thought it was the chemicals in the cigarette.
M: No, the chemicals only make smokers want to smoke more, and also destroy your body. There's really nothing good inside cigarettes at all. They are filled with poison.
W: You're right. People should really give up smoking. Smokers smell bad because of cigarettes too.

W: 담배 가격이 다시 오른대.
M: 그거 좋은 소식인걸. 어쨌든 담배는 피우지 말아야 해. 건강에 아주 해로워.
W: 맞아, 하지만 너무 많은 사람들이 아직도 담배를 피워.
M: 사람들이 담배를 끊어야 하는데. 담배에는 좋은 게 하나도 없거든.
W: 글쎄, 흡연가들은 담배가 스트레스를 완화시키고 마음을 가라앉히는데 도움을 준다고 하더라.
M: 그건 절대로 담배 때문이 아니야. 담배를 피우는 데 드는 시간 때문에 그런거야. 담배는 정말이지 마음을 가라앉히는 거랑 전혀 상관이 없어.
W: 진짜? 나는 그게 담배 속의 화학 물질 때문이라고 생각했는데.
M: 아니야, 화학 물질은 사람들이 더 담배를 피우게만 할 뿐 아니라 몸을 망가뜨리지. 담배에는 정말 좋은 것이 전혀 없어. 독만 가득할 뿐이야.
W: 네 말이 옳아. 사람들은 정말 담배를 끊어야 해. 흡연가들한테는 담배 때문에 냄새도 나거든.

iBT Practice 1 p.160

1. (A)   2. (A), (C)   3. (B)

Listen to part of a conversation between two friends.

M: I have to write an essay about a country's culture.
W: Really? Which country are you going to write about?
M: I'm deciding on whether to write on Canada or the US. It seems like they have very different systems of mixing cultures.
W: What do you mean? Aren't the two countries really close together?

M: Yes, the two countries are close, but very different in what they believe. The US believes in a system called the "melting pot."

W: Does that mean that they melt the cultures or something like that?

M: I guess you could say that. The US wants everyone to mix and create one big culture. That's to say, the Americans think that it will bring everyone closer together, and everyone will have the same culture as others.

W: How about Canada? Do they mix cultures together?

M: Yes, Canada also mixes cultures together, but they call their system the "salad bowl toss." They do not want people in their country to forget their culture. Canadians think that this system respects all the different cultures in the country.

W: 🎧 Wow, both of them sound correct. I guess it will be hard to say which country is correct. Sorry, but I have to go. **I hope you make the right choice.**

M: 나는 한 나라의 문화에 대한 글을 써야 돼.

W: 정말? 어떤 나라에 대해서 쓸 거야?

M: 캐나다에 대해 쓸 것인지 미국에 대해 쓸 것인지 생각하고 있는 중이야. 두 나라는 다른 나라의 문화를 수용하는데 매우 다른 태도를 갖은 것처럼 보여.

W: 무슨 뜻이야? 두 나라는 서로 매우 가까이 있지 않아?

M: 맞아, 가까이 있지, 그렇지만 그들이 생각하는 것에 있어서는 매우 달라. 미국은 "melting pot"라고 불리는 시스템을 갖고 있어.

W: 여러 다른 문화를 녹였다는 뜻이니?

M: 그렇게도 말할 수 있을 거 같아. 미국은 모든 문화가 섞여져서 하나의 큰 문화를 만들어내고 싶어해. 말하자면, 미국인들은 그게 모든 사람을 함께 더 가까이 모은다고 생각해. 그리고 그 사람들은 다른 사람들과 같은 문화를 갖는 거지.

W: 캐나다는 어때? 캐나다도 여러 문화들이 섞여있어?

M: 응, 캐나다도 문화가 섞여 있는데 그 시스템을 "salad bowl toss"라고 불러. 캐나다는 사람들이 자신의 나라 문화를 잊어버리는 것을 원하지 않아. 그들은 이 시스템이 다른 모든 문화를 존중한다고 생각해.

W: 우와, 두 가지 다 일리가 있게 들리네. 어떤 나라가 옳다고 말하기는 어려울 거 같아. 미안한데, 나 가봐야겠어. 잘 결정해서 써라.

iBT Practice 2  p.162

1. (D) 2. (A) 3. (B)

Listen to part of a talk in a social studies class.

Non-profit organizations help people without earning any money at all. All the members and companies involved in these organizations are volunteers. Some even use their own money when working in these organizations. There are many types of non-profit organizations.

An example of a large organization that helps other people is the International Red Cross. The International Red Cross is involved in many things. They are like an emergency hospital, with many doctors and nurses. **Q5** 🎧 The organization helps countries around the world in emergencies. They provide food and shelter in these countries. They also collect blood during their free time, **although it is hard to imagine that they have any free time at all.**

Non-profit organizations can also help animals and plants. There is an organization called Greenpeace that works to protect the environment. Another non-profit organization called the World Wildlife Fund protects animals in the wild. Both these organizations have thousands of members all over the world, and everyone in these organizations works very hard.

Q6 🎧 **No matter what kind of organization, the most important part is the volunteers that help others. Therefore, if all of us help a little, the world will certainly become a better place.**

비영리단체는 전혀 돈을 벌지 않고 사람들을 돕는다. 이러한 단체에 관련된 모든 사람들이나 회사들은 자원 봉사자다. 어떤 사람은 이러한 단체에서 일할 때 자신의 돈을 사용하기도 한다. 많은 형태의 비영리단체가 있다.

국제적십자는 사람들을 돕는 큰 단체의 한 예이다. 국제적십자는 많은 일을 하고 있다. 이 단체는 많은 의사와 간호사가 있는 응급 병원과 같다. 이 곳은 비상상황에 처해 있는 세계의 나라들을 돕는다. 이러한 나라들에게 음식과 잠자리를 제공한다. 자유 시간이 있을 것이라 상상하기는 어렵지만 시간이 있는 동안에는 혈액을 모은다.

비영리단체는 또한 동물과 식물을 돕는다. 환경 보호를 위해 활동하는 그린피스라는 단체가 있다. 또 다른 비영리단체로는 야생동물을 보호하는 세계야생생물기금이 있다. 이 두 단체는 세계 곳곳에 수천 명의 회원들이 있고, 단체의 모든 사람들이 매우 열심히 일한다.

단체의 종류와 상관없이 가장 중요한 것은 다른 사람을 돕는 자원 봉사자들이다. 그러므로, 만약 우리가 조금씩 도와준다면 세상은 확실히 좀더 나은 곳이 될 것이다.

Word Review
p.166

1. overseas
2. destroy
3. volunteer
4. shelter
5. recycle
6. donate
7. emergency
8. independence
9. are involved in
10. throw away
11. on time
12. is responsible for

Mini Test 1

p.170

1. (B)	2. (C)	3. (A)	4. (D)
5. (B)	6. (A)	7. (B)	8. (C)
9. Yes: (B), (C) / No: (A), (D)			10. (A)
11. (B)	12. (A)		

1-4.

Listen to part of a conversation between two friends.

M: Do you have any idea when the first clock was invented?

W: 🎧 It's a bit hard to say. The first clocks that we know of, according to history, were called sundials.

M: A sundial? Are you sure?

W: Yes, a sundial uses the sun to tell us what time it is. The shadow of the sun can tell us what time it is. There was a slight problem with this, because it only worked when the sun was up.

M: That would have been very inconvenient. So when was the first mechanical clock invented?

W: People think that a monk made the first mechanical clock around the year 1000 AD. He made the clock so that he knew when to pray.

M: Wow, so the clock is quite old then. So when did people start carrying around smaller clocks?

W: You mean watches? I heard that they were made during the 1500s in Germany. They were still very big and heavy, compared to our wrist watches. In fact, just 100 years ago, people only had pocket watches.

M: Oh, I've seen those in the movies. People are always winding them by hand.

M: 처음으로 시계가 발명된 것이 언제였는지 너는 혹시 아니?

W: 잘은 모르겠어. 역사에 따르면 우리가 알고있는 최초의 시계는 해시계였어.

M: 해시계? 확실한 거야?

W: 그래, 해시계는 해를 이용해서 시간을 우리에게 알려주지. 해가 만드는 그림자를 봐서 우리는 시간을 파악할 수 있는 거야. 하지만 약간의 문제가 있었지. 왜냐하면 해가 있을 때에만 효과가 있었기 때문이야.

M: 정말 불편했겠는걸. 그럼 기계로 된 시계는 언제 발명된 거지?

W: 사람들은 1000년쯤에 어떤 수도승이 첫 기계 시계를 발명했다고 하지. 기도 할 시간을 알기 위해 시계를 만들었다고 해.

M: 아, 그럼 시계는 꽤 오래되었구나. 그럼 사람들은 언제부터 시계를 갖고 다니게 되었지?

W: 손목 시계 말하는 거야? 1500년대쯤에 독일에서 만들어졌다고 들었어. 그 때 시계들은 오늘 우리의 손목 시계에 비해 아주 크고 무거웠지. 사실 100년 전에 사람들은 회중시계만 갖고 있었어.

M: 아, 난 그런 시계들 영화에서 봤어. 사람들은 주로 손으로 태엽을 감고 그랬지.

5-8.

Listen to part of a talk in a history class.

Greece has always been related to poems and mystical creatures. This is due to the many philosophers and wise poets in Greece during the olden days. One of the people who wrote mythical stories and Greek mythology was a brilliant blind poet named Homer at about 700 BC. His two very exciting poems, The Odyssey and The Iliad, are considered masterpieces even today.

The first poem was called The Iliad and is about the Trojan War. The war was between the Greeks and the Trojans. The story talks about how the Greeks tricked the Trojans by hiding inside a large wooden horse. The Trojans did not know that there were Greeks inside the horse. The Trojans brought it into their castle. Therefore, the Greeks won the war in the end.

The second poem was The Odyssey, a continuing story of The Iliad. The story is about a Greek soldier called Odysseus, who takes 10 years to get back home after the battle with the Trojans. It is said Odysseus was one of the soldiers who hid in the Trojan horse. Some even say it was Odysseus that thought of building the horse. During his trip back home, he meets many other fictional Greek characters like the one-eyed giant, Cyclops.

그리스는 항상 시와 신비로운 생물체들과 연관되어왔다. 이것은 옛날에 그리스에 살던 많은 철학자들과 슬기로운 시인들 때문이다. 기원전 700년경에 신화를 이용한 이야기들과 그리스 신화를 쓴 사람들 중에 호머라는 아주 훌륭한 맹인 시인이 있었다. 그의 흥미로운 두 시, 오딧세이와 일리아드는 오늘날까지도 대작으로 인정을 받는다.

첫 번째 시는 일리아드라고 불리우고 트로이 전쟁을 다루고 있다. 이 전쟁은 그리스 사람들과 트로이 사람들 사이에 벌어진 것이었다. 이 이야기는 커다란 나무 말에 그리스인들이 숨어서 트로이인들을 어떻게 속였는지에 대한 것이다. 트로이 사람들은 말 속에 그리스 사람들이 있는 것을 전혀 몰랐다. 그들은 말을 그들의 성벽 안으로 들여왔다. 그리고 그리스인들은 결국에 전쟁에서 승리를 거두었다.

두 번째 시는 일리아드에 이어지는 이야기인 오딧세이였다. 이 이야기에서는 트로이 전쟁이 끝나고 10년 후에 집에 돌아가게 된 오딧세이우스 라는 전사가 나온다. 트로이의 목마 속에 숨은 병사들 중 한 명이었다고 한다. 어떤 사람들은 오딧세이우스가 트로이의 목마를 만들 것을 생각해냈다고 주장하기도 한다. 그가 집에 돌아오는 길에 눈 하나 달린 거인 사이클롭스 같은 가상의 그리스 인물들을 만나게 된다.

9-12.

Listen to part of a discussion in a science class.

T: Insects are the toughest animals in the world. They have excellent survival methods. They can live anywhere in the world.

W: Aren't camels the best survivors? They can live without water for a month in the desert.

M: I think she's correct.

T: Yes, camels are good survivors, but insects are much better survivors in a variety of environments. Some say that the cockroach is one of the toughest.

W: Yuck, I hate cockroaches.

M: Well, how do people judge which animal or insect is toughest?

T: Probably by comparing how long they have been around in this world. There are quite a few insects that have not changed at all for millions of years.

M: Quite a few? Could you tell us another one?

T: 🎧 Of course. Scorpions have been around

for a few hundred million years. They are really tough creatures. They can even live when frozen in ice. When the ice melts, the scorpions walk away as if nothing happened.

W: Are you serious? I guess you can't beat that.
T: Yes, it is an amazing insect. Scorpions also do not drink water at all, as they get all the water they need from the food they eat. And speaking of food, scorpions can live without food for a year!
M: Wow, they sure are tough animals.

T: 곤충들은 세상에서 가장 강한 동물이라고 볼 수 있단다. 그들은 뛰어난 생존 방법들을 갖고 있지. 세상 아무 곳에나 살 수 있어.
W: 낙타들이 제일 생존 능력이 뛰어나지 않나요? 그들은 사막에서 한 달 동안 물을 마시지 않고 살 수 있잖아요.
M: 얘 말이 맞는 것 같아요.
T: 그래, 낙타들도 생존 능력이 뛰어나지만 곤충들은 다양한 환경에서 더욱 더 잘 살아나갈 수 있단다. 어떤 사람들은 바퀴벌레들이 제일 강하다고 말하지.
W: 윽, 난 바퀴벌레들이 제일 싫은데.
M: 그럼 사람들은 어떤 동물이나 곤충이 제일 강하다는 것을 어떻게 판단할 수 있는 거죠?
T: 아마 그 동물들이 이 세상에 얼마 동안 살아왔는지를 비교해서 할 수 있을 거야. 몇 백만 년 동안 전혀 변하지 않고 살아온 곤충들이 꽤 있으니깐.
M: 꽤 있다고요? 또 다른 것에 대해 얘기를 해주실 수 있나요?
T: 물론이지. 전갈들은 지금까지 몇 백만 년 동안 지구에 살아왔단다. 그들은 정말 강한 생물이야. 전갈들은 얼음 속에 얼려있는 상태에서도 살수 있어. 얼음이 녹으면 전갈들은 아무 일이 없었다는 듯이 나와서 기어 다니지.
W: 그게 사실인가요? 그것보다 강한 것은 없겠네요.
T: 그래, 정말 대단한 곤충이지. 전갈들은 섭취하는 음식에 있는 수분이 그들에겐 충분해서 아예 물을 마시지 않아. 그리고 음식 얘기가 나왔으니 말인데, 그들은 아무것도 섭취하지 않아도 일년을 그냥 살 수 있단다.
M: 와, 정말 강한 곤충들이네요.

Mini Test 2

p.176

1. (C)	2. (D)	3. (A)	4. (D)
5. (D)	6. (A)	7. (B)	8. (C)
9. (A)	10. (A), (B)	11. (D)	12. (B)

1-4.

Listen to part of a conversation between a student and a librarian.

M: Excuse me. I have something to ask you.
W: Sure, how can I help you?
M: Well, I was cleaning up my room the other day, and I found an old library book that I forgot to return.
W: Oh, don't worry. Many people go through the same thing. Could you give me the book so I can scan the label?
M: Oh, that is another problem. Half of the label tore off. I'm really sorry about it.
W: Oh, that would be a bit of a problem. How long have you had the book?
M: I am not very sure, probably for about 1 or 2 months.
W: Hmmm ... Well, let's start with your name. I'm sure we still have a record of it in the computer somewhere.
M: Yes, my name is John Smith.
W: Let's see. Oh, we have 4 people under the name of John Smith. What is the title of the book?
M: The Pearl, by John Steinbeck.
W: 🎧 Alright, I found it. You borrowed it over 3 months ago. The computer says that your fine is $10. That's the maximum amount.
M: That's it? Thank you for helping me out. Here's the money and the book.

M: 실례합니다. 물어 볼게 있는데요.
W: 뭘 도와줄까?
M: 제가 저번 날 제 방을 정리하고 있었는데, 반납하는 것을 잊

은 도서관 책을 찾았어요.
W: 아, 걱정 안 해도 돼. 많은 사람들이 비슷한 일을 겪는단다. 라벨을 스캔 할 수 있게 책을 줄래?
M: 문제가 있어요. 라벨 반이 뜯어져 버렸어요. 정말 죄송해요.
W: 아, 그러면 약간 문제가 될 수 있겠네. 책을 얼마 동안 갖고 있었지?
M: 확실하진 않지만, 아마 한 두 달 동안 갖고 있었을 거에요.
W: 흠… 그럼 이름부터 시작해야겠네. 아마 컴퓨터 어딘가엔 기록이 남아있을 거야.
M: 네, 제 이름은 존 스미스 입니다.
W: 어디보자. 동명이인이 네 명이 있네. 책의 제목이 뭐지?
M: 존 스타인벡이 쓴 〈진주〉라는 소설이에요.
W: 찾았다. 세 달 전에 빌려갔구나. 컴퓨터에는 벌금이 10달러라고 나오네. 그게 최고 벌금이다.
M: 그게 다예요? 도와주셔서 너무 감사해요. 여기 돈과 책이 있어요.

5 - 8.

Listen to part of a talk in a music class.

People call music the universal language. We do not have to understand languages or numbers to appreciate music. Many cultures in the world have their own music. There are many types of music, and some music does not even need musical instruments.

A new type of music that does not involve traditional musical instruments is gaining popularity in Korea. The performance is called "Nanta." "Nanta" makes music by using common things we find in our homes. For example, they hit big water barrels, or tap cutting boards with knives to make beats. It is so popular that they have even performed on Broadway, the most famous opera stage in the US.

Another type of music is called "a capella." "A capella" is music made by a group of people that use only their voices. The "a capella" style originated in Italy to make music in churches before organs were invented. 🎧 It is very popular around the world, but it takes a lot of practice and co-ordination to be good in "a capella." Some "a capella" groups perform in the streets, and there are always people that are happy to hear them.

사람들은 음악을 세계 공통어라고 한다. 음악을 감상하기 위해 따로 언어나 숫자를 이해해야 할 필요가 없다. 지구의 많은 문화는 각각의 음악을 갖고 있다. 많은 음악의 종류가 있고 어떤 음악은 악기를 이용하지 않는다.

한국에서는 전통적인 악기를 사용하지 않는 새로운 형식의 음악이 인기를 얻고 있다. 그것은 "난타"라고 불리운다. "난타"는 집에서 흔히 찾을 수 있는 물건들로 음악을 만든다. 예를 들어서, 장단을 만들기 위해 큰 물통을 치거나, 칼로 도마를 두들긴다. 너무 인기가 많아서 그들은 미국에 있는 유명한 오페라 무대인 브로드웨이에서도 공연을 한 적이 있다.

또 다른 종류의 음악은 "아카펠라" 이다. "아카펠라" 는 사람들이 오직 그들의 음성으로만 음악을 만드는 것이다. "아카펠라" 스타일은 오르간이 발명되기 전에 교회에서 음악을 만들기 위해 이태리에서 생겨난 것이다. 세계적으로 인기가 있고 구성원의 많은 노력과 조화를 통해서만이 "아카펠라"를 멋지게 할 수 있다. 어떤 "아카펠라" 그룹들은 거리에서도 공연하고 이것을 듣게 되면 너무 행복해 하는 사람들이 항상 있다.

9 - 12.

Listen to part of a discussion in a class.

T: What do you think about wearing uniforms to school?
W: I think it's great that we have uniforms to wear.
M: Not for me. I like to be different from others.
W: 🎧 Oh, I have those days too, but I don't think it is that bad. It can be very stressful to think of what to wear the next day. We'd have to buy more clothes. With uniforms, there is no worry about what to wear.
M: I see your point, but I still prefer choosing what to wear.
T: Both of you have a point. Uniforms can be good or bad, like anything else in life. In reality, most students around the world have to wear uniforms.
W: I was always curious to know why students must wear uniforms.
T: There are a few reasons for this. Uniforms help students focus on their studies and not waste time worrying about clothes. It also stops students from trying to show off to others by wearing expensive clothes.
M: But that could be part of expressing ourselves. Also, some of the uniforms can be expensive as well. Finally, the uniform design or color can be

suitable for girls, but maybe not for boys.

T: 학교에 교복을 입고 오는 것에 대해 어떻게 생각하니?
W: 저는 교복을 입는 것이 좋다고 생각해요.
M: 저는 아니에요. 전 남들과 좀 달랐으면 좋겠어요.
W: 음, 나도 그런 날들이 있긴 하지만, 그래도 교복은 그리 나쁘지 않아. 다음 날 뭘 입어야 할 지 고민하는 것도 스트레스가 이만 저만이 아닐 수 있잖아. 그리고 옷을 더 많이 사야겠지. 교복이 있어서 무엇을 입어야 할지 걱정을 하지 않잖아.
M: 네 말에도 일리가 있지만, 그래도 나는 무얼 입을지 고르는 게 더 낫겠어.
T: 둘 다 맞는 의견들이다. 인생의 모든 것처럼, 교복에도 좋은 점과 나쁜 점들이 있지. 현실적으로 대부분의 학생들은 현재 교복을 학교에서 입어야 해.
W: 전 항상 학생들이 왜 교복을 입어야 하는지에 대해 궁금했었어요.
T: 이것에는 여러 가지 이유가 있어. 교복은 학생들이 공부에 더욱 집중할 수 있도록 도와주고 옷에 대해 신경을 쓰지 않게 하지. 그리고 비싼 옷을 입은 학생들이 잘난 체하는 것도 방지하구.
M: 하지만 그것은 우리 자신들을 표현하는 것일 수 있잖아요. 그리고 교복도 값이 비쌀 수 있어요. 마지막으로 교복의 디자인이나 색깔이 여학생들에게는 잘 어울릴지 몰라도 남학생들에게는 그리 잘 어울리지 않아요.

Mini Test 3

p.182

1. (D)   2. Yes: (A), (C) / No: (B), (D)
3. (C)   4. (B)   5. (B)
6. Yes: (A), (B) / No: (C), (D)   7. (A)
8. (D)   9. (B)   10. (C)   11. (C)
12. (B)

1-4.

Listen to part of a conversation between two students.

M: I'm going to Paris next month. Do you know anything about that city?
W: Wow, that's fantastic! I was there last year. I know that the streets of Paris are more romantic than other streets of the world. You should visit the Eiffel Tower and the Arc de Triomphe too.
M: Really? Which romantic street are you talking about?
W: The road next to the Seine River. Many couples go there for a date.
M: How about the two places you mentioned?
W: Well, the Eiffel Tower is the symbol of France. The top floor of the tower has a very famous and romantic restaurant. You should try the food; it's great.
M: That sounds wonderful. And what was the other place?
W: The Arc de Triomphe. It is a building that was made to remember Napoleon as a successful general. You can walk inside the building. The walls have names of many soldiers who died in wars.
M: You know so much about Paris. Do you want to go together? I don't want to be lost in a foreign country.
W: What a great idea! I'd love to go to Paris again.
M: 나 다음달에 파리에 가. 너 혹시 그 도시에 대해서 좀 아는 거 있니?

W: 우와, 굉장한 걸! 나는 작년에 거기 갔었어. 파리의 거리는 세계의 다른 어떤 거리보다도 낭만적이지. 에펠탑과 개선문은 꼭 가봐야 한다구.
M: 정말? 어느 낭만적인 거리를 말하는 거니?
W: 세느강 옆에 있는 거리지. 많은 커플들이 데이트하러 그곳으로 가지.
M: 네가 말한 그 두 곳은 어때?
W: 음, 에펠탑은 파리의 상징이지. 그 탑의 꼭대기 층에는 아주 유명하고 낭만적인 레스토랑이 있어. 거기 음식을 꼭 먹어봐. 정말 맛있어.
M: 정말 멋지겠는걸. 그리고 다른 한 군데는?
W: 개선문이야. 그 건물은 나폴레옹을 위대한 장군으로 기억하기 위해 지어졌어. 건물 안을 걸어 다닐 수도 있어. 벽에는 전쟁에서 죽은 군인들의 이름이 적혀있어.
M: 파리에 대해서 아는 게 많구나. 너도 같이 가지 않을래? 외국에서 길을 잃어버리고 싶진 않거든.
W: 좋은 생각인데! 나도 파리에 다시 가고 싶어.

5 - 8.

Listen to part of a talk in a biology class.

There are many animals that live in the water. But there are not many animals that live under water when they are young, and then live on land when they are older. One such animal is the frog. It has an amazing life cycle.

First, the mother frog lays thousands of eggs in the water. The eggs have a very slippery surface to protect the babies inside the eggs. The babies come out, and for the first three weeks they grow a mouth, tail, gills and eyes. Gills are what fish use to breathe under water.

Then, the tadpoles start growing small legs. They become better swimmers with a longer tail and start looking for food. Their legs grow longer, and they also start to grow hands.

After three months, the tadpoles come out of the water and become young frogs. The gills disappear, and the young frogs start breathing with lungs. The young frogs start jumping around to move and start to catch food with their very long tongue. After three years, the adult frogs are ready to lay new eggs in the water.

물속에서 사는 동물들은 많이 있다. 하지만 어릴 때는 물속에서 생활하고 다 자라면 물 밖으로 나오는 동물들은 많지 않다. 그런 동물로는 개구리를 들 수 있다. 개구리의 성장 주기는 아주 놀랍다.

먼저 어미 개구리는 물속에 수 천 개의 알을 낳는다. 알은 속의 아기들을 보호하기 위해 아주 미끄러운 막으로 덮여있다. 새끼는 부화되면 처음 3주 동안에 입, 꼬리, 아가미, 눈이 생긴다. 아가미는 어류들이 물속에서 숨을 쉬기 위해 사용하는 기관이다.

그 후에 올챙이들은 작은 뒷다리가 자라기 시작한다. 긴 꼬리를 갖고 더 잘 헤엄쳐서 먹이를 찾아 나서기 시작한다. 뒷다리가 점점 커지면 앞다리도 자란다.

3개월 후에 올챙이는 물 밖으로 나와 어린 개구리가 된다. 아가미는 사라지고 어린 개구리는 허파로 숨을 쉰다. 어린 개구리는 점프를 해서 이동을 하고 아주 긴 혀로 먹이를 잡아 먹기 시작한다. 3년이 지나 성장한 개구리는 새로운 알을 물속에 낳을 준비를 한다.

9 - 12.

Listen to part of a discussion in a gym class.

T: What do you think is the oldest sport in the world?
W: Isn't it running? I'm sure people have been running for a very long time.
M: I don't think so. There must be something else.
T: Some argue that the oldest sport in the world is wrestling. People found drawings of wrestling in caves, believed to be over 20,000 years old.
W: I disagree. I'm sure humans have been running even before that.
M: My point is that the meaning of sports is doing something for fun. Humans must have run to hunt or hide.
W: 🎧 Humans could have been running for fun too. Maybe they did not have time to draw because they were having fun running.
M: Come on. Wrestling was an event in the ancient Olympics held in Athens thousands of years ago. It has been a popular sport for so long.
W: But the most popular sport in the ancient Olympics was running. I still say running could be the oldest sport.

T: 세계에서 가장 오래된 경기가 뭐라고 생각하니?
W: 달리기 아니에요? 분명히 사람들은 아주 오래 전부터 달리기를 해왔을 거예요.
M: 난 그렇게 생각하지 않아. 다른 뭔가가 틀림없이 있을거야.
T: 어떤 사람들은 세계에서 가장 오래된 경기가 레슬링이라고

하지. 사람들이 동굴에서 레슬링 그림을 발견했는데 2만년 이상 된 걸로 예측하거든.
W: 제 생각은 달라요. 인류는 그 이전부터 달리기를 해왔을 거에요.
M: 내 요지는 스포츠란 즐거움을 위해 뭔가를 한다는 뜻이야. 사람들은 그저 사냥을 하거나 숨기위해 달려야 했다는 거지.
W: 재미로 달리기를 했을 수도 있어. 달리기를 하느라 재미있어서 그림 그릴 시간이 없었던 거지.
M: 무슨 소리야. 레슬링은 수 천년 전 아테네에서 있었던 고대 올림픽에서 한 종목이었어. 그렇게 오래 전부터 인기 있는 스포츠였어.
W: 하지만 고대 올림픽에서 가장 인기 있던 종목은 달리기였어. 난 달리기가 제일 오래된 스포츠라고 생각해.

LinguaForum TOEFL® *i*BT Series eBasic - e - b - m - i - Hooked On

Junior Series

- *i*BT eBasic TOEFL® Reading / Listening
- *i*BT e TOEFL® Reading / Listening / Grammar
- *i*BT b TOEFL® Reading / Listening / Writing / Grammar

Test Prep.

Intermediate Level

- TOEFL® *i*BT m-Reading / m-Listening / m-Writing / m-Speaking
- New Edition TOEFL® *i*BT i-Reading / i-Listening / i-Writing / i-Speaking
- TOEFL® *i*BT Core Topic Guide Series / **Intro Vocabulary**

Advanced Level

- **New Edition Hooked On TOEFL®** Reading / Listening / Writing / Speaking
- **Frequency#1 TOEFL® Vocabulary**
- **TOEFL® *i*BT INSIDER** – The Super Guide / **TOEFL® *i*BT Test Book I**

LinguaForum™

우133-120, 서울특별시 성동구 광나루로 310 푸조비즈타워 5F
교재주문 (02) 3480-6627 대표전화 590-6900
● www.linguaforum.com 회사 소개·도서 문의 및 상담

시험 상세 : 시험 화면은 다음과 같이 구성되었습니다.

Reading
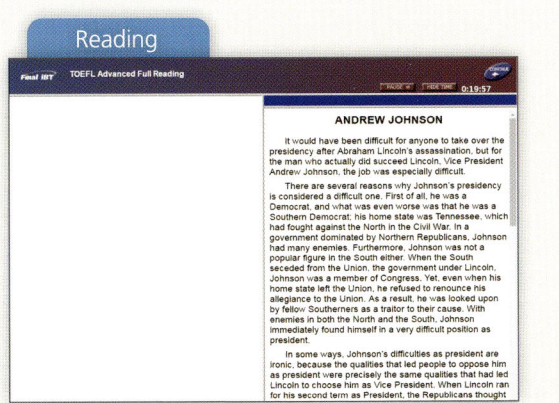
학술적인 내용의 지문을 이해하는 능력을 평가합니다.

Listening

강의, 교실 토론 및 대화를 듣고 이해하는 능력을 평가합니다.

Speaking
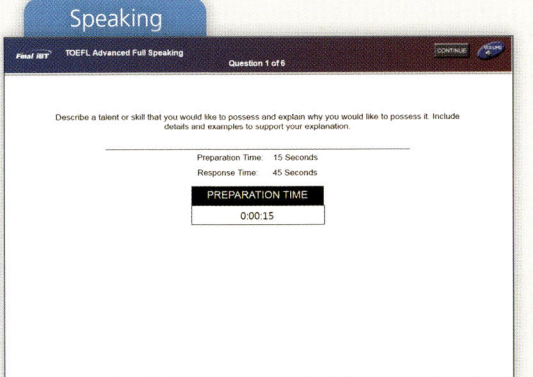
다양한 주제에 대해 말할 수 있는 능력을 평가합니다.

Writing
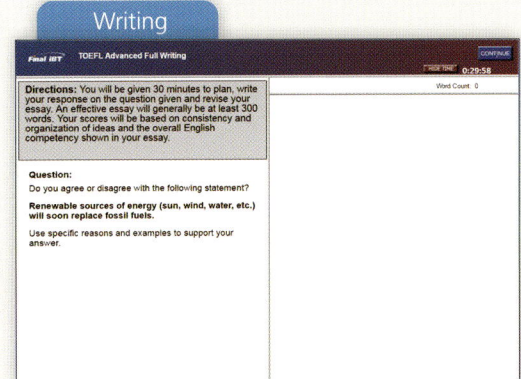
강의내용을 요약하고 자신의 의견을 정리하는 작문능력을 평가합니다.

성적표

각각의 모의 테스트를 마친 후 **예상점수를 확인**할 수 있습니다. SPEAKING과 WRITING 점수는 **채점 전문 인력**에 의해 매겨집니다.

시험 준비 세팅

먼저, 마이크가 있는 헤드셋을 준비해주세요.
그리고 인터넷이 연결된 상태에서 크롬브라우저로 접속하여 시험에 응시하시면 됩니다.

시험 응시 및 문의 사항 Tel : **02-3483-2786**

초급부터 실전까지 토플교재의 바이블
링구아포럼 TOEFL Series

- 아시아 최초로 2003년부터 미국은 물론 전 세계로 영어 교재와 판권 수출
- 온라인 서점 아마존닷컴 토플 판매 1위 (2003년, 2004년)
- 주니어 토플 개념 정의
- 최초 6단계별 토플 시리즈 개발

링구아포럼의 6단계별 토플 교재 **eBASIC / e / b / m / i / Hooked on / Insider / Test Book**
– eBasic 시리즈를 시작으로 e, b, m, i, Hooked On 순으로 단계가 올라갑니다. 영문 종합서 Insider 와 모의고사집 Test Book이 있습니다.

1 단계 — New Edition eBasic Series
중학교 1~2학년 수준으로 토플을 처음 접하는 학습자를 위한 입문 단계로, iBT의 주제와 형식, 문제유형에 입문 수준의 어휘와 문법으로 구성되었습니다.

〈개정판〉

2 단계 — New Edition e Series
중학교 2~3학년 수준의 토플 학습자를 위해 개발된 두번째 초급 단계이며, iBT의 주제와 형식, 문제유형에 입문 수준의 어휘와 문법으로 구성되었습니다.

〈개정판〉

3 단계 — b Series
중학교 3학년 이상의 영어능력을 가진 학습자를 대상으로 개발. 링구아포럼 eBasic, e 시리즈를 학습한 학습자에서부터, 토플을 처음 접하는 대학생/성인들 모두 토플에 적응하고 중급~고급 단계로 진입할 수 있도록 구성 되었습니다.

4 단계 — m Series
중급 수준(성인 입문)의 토플 학습자를 대상으로 개발. iBT에 등장하는 모든 주제와 문제유형 등을 모두 다루었으며, 실전보다 조금 쉬운 수준으로 연습할 수 있습니다.

〈개정판〉

   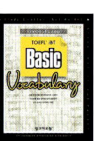

5 단계 — New Edition i Series
실제 토플 시험을 준비하는 학습자를 대상으로 개발. 링구아포럼 토플 시리즈의 중/고급단계로, iBT에 등장하는 모든 주제와 문제유형 등을 모두 다루었으며, 실전과 거의 유사한 수준으로 연습할 수 있습니다.

6 단계 — New Edition Hooked On Series
실제 토플 시험을 준비하는 학습자를 대상으로 한 고급단계로, iBT에 등장하는 모든 주제와 문제유형등을 모두 다루어, 실전과 동일한 수준으로 연습할 수 있습니다.

Level Chart

Lingua Forum

Beginning	Intermediate	Advanced

Elementary

Secondary

Test Prep

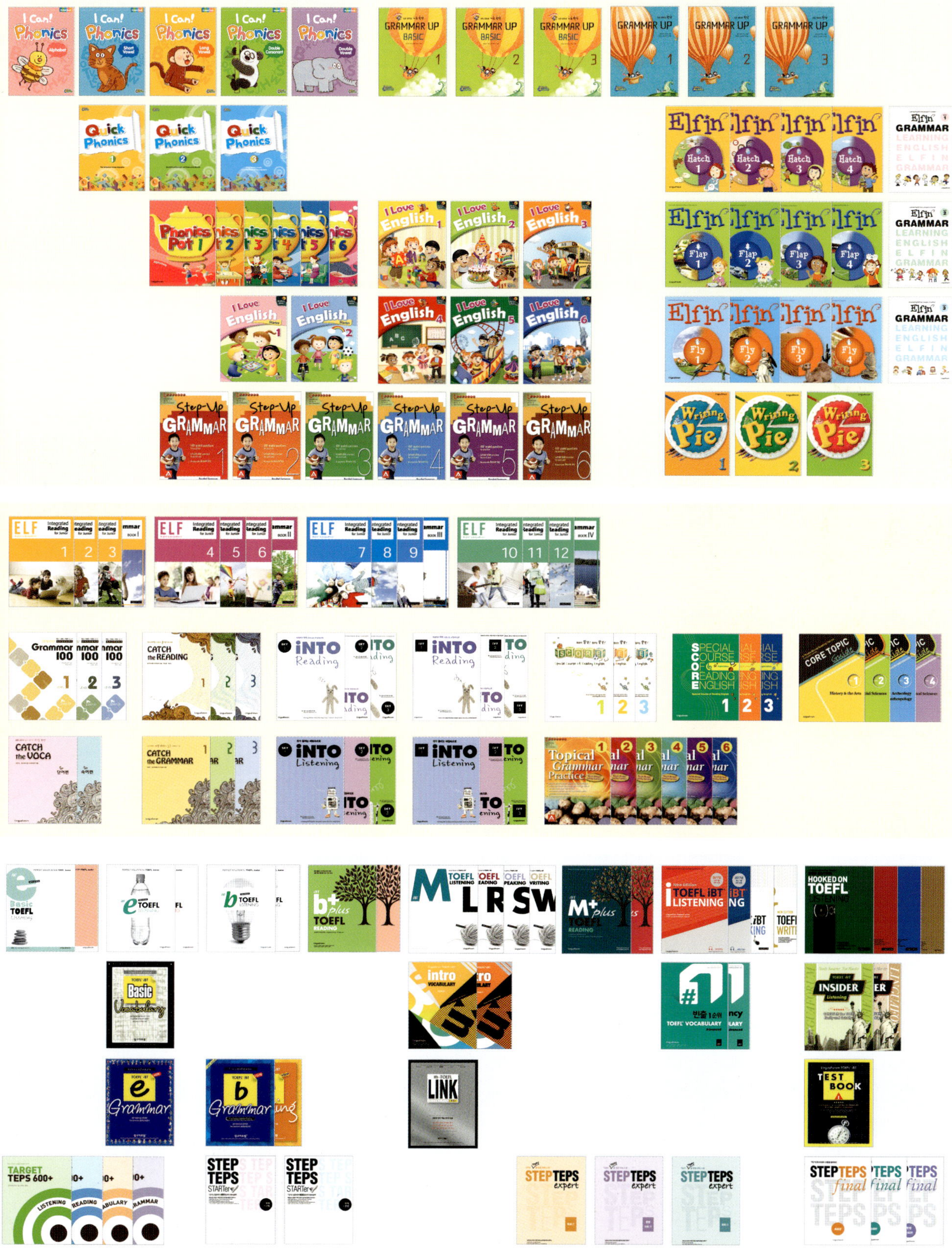

LinguaForum TOEFL® iBT Series eBasic - e - b - m - i - Hooked On

Junior Series

*i*BT eBasic TOEFL® Reading / Listening
*i*BT e TOEFL® Reading / Listening / Grammar
*i*BT b TOEFL® Reading / Listening / Writing / Grammar

Test Prep.

Intermediate Level

TOEFL® *i*BT m-Reading / m-Listening / m-Writing / m-Speaking
New Edition TOEFL® *i*BT i-Reading / i-Listening / i-Writing / i-Speaking
TOEFL® *i*BT Core Topic Guide Series / Intro Vocabulary

Advanced Level

New Edition Hooked On TOEFL® Reading / Listening / Writing / Speaking
Frequency#1 TOEFL® Vocabulary
TOEFL® *i*BT INSIDER – The Super Guide / TOEFL® *i*BT Test Book I

가격 19,000원

우133-120, 서울특별시 성동구 광나루로 310 푸조비즈타워 5F
교재주문 (02) 3480-6627 대표전화 590-6900
● www.linguaforum.com 회사 소개·도서 문의 및 상담

ISBN 978-89-5563-628-4